I0797292

The Ultimate Cookie HANDBOOK

The Ultimate Cookie HANDBOOK

Your Guide to Baking Perfect Cookies Every Time

ISBN: 978-0-578-63666-5 (Hardcover)

Book design LeAnna Weller Smith

Printed in China

First published 2020.

Fourth Edition
First Printing

Published by Tessa Arias
www.handletheheat.com

To my family for always supporting me, to my friends for always encouraging me, and to everyone in the Handle the Heat community who loves dessert and the magic of baking.

Contents

Introduction

"What went wrong? Why did my cookies turn out this way?"

I get asked those questions and many others daily. Over the years on HandletheHeat.com I've shared many cookie recipes and have done tons of experimenting with the science behind baking. When I published my Ultimate Guide to Chocolate Chip Cookies in 2013, it went viral and the article has now been visited over half a million times. Clearly people love their cookies. What people love even more is an *incredible* cookie, which can be challenging to create consistently. On my website I host a monthly baking challenge where I encourage everyone in my audience to bake the same recipe, snap a photo, and share their results. The first time we all baked the same cookie recipe I was astounded by how different some batches of cookies looked from the others. Take a peek for yourself:

Audience photos from the August 2019 Baking Challenge, featuring the Soft Batch Chocolate Chip Cookies on page 99

Even when everyone follows the exact same recipe, the results can vary widely. That's why I decided to write this book. I wanted to show you how and why your kitchen results can vary. Why your cookies might not turn out like the photo in the book, magazine, or website. Or why the recipe you made months ago with stellar results didn't turn out the same when you made it last week. Or why your cookies haven't been the same since you moved to a new place.

I wanted to answer every question I've been asked, all in one convenient place. To give you the tools you need to enter the kitchen with confidence, like I'm right there beside you. With this book as your guide, you can become the expert. I hope you'll view this as your cookie bible, with everything you need to know to create your perfect version of any cookie recipe and delight your friends, family, and taste buds. You will soon understand how to make any cookie more chewy, soft, cakey, crisp, thick, thin, or whatever your heart desires. With this knowledge, you'll even be able to get closer to replicating the cookies from your favorite bakery or from your grandma's lost recipe. No more failures, only huge successes, and best of all, you don't need to be a science whiz or professional baker to get there. You'll finally be able to create your go-to perfected recipes that everyone will beg you to share.

Producing this book involved countless hours in the kitchen, pounds of sugar, and more dirty dishes than I care to remember. I baked up many dozens of purposefully mediocre or even horrible cookies to capture the baking science at work. I was more than willing to make the sacrifice so I could share the results with you. I'm so excited for you to get your hands on the coming pages. I think you'll love them and I hope you will enjoy all the tips, tricks, secrets, and recipes I'm sharing with you!

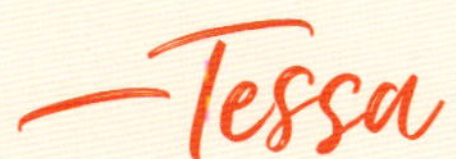

Pressure Cooker
Cookies & CREAM

My Baking Journey

Neither of my parents and none of my grandparents like to bake. In fact, I have a fond and hilarious childhood memory of attempting to make a box cake mix with my beloved grandmother. I don't know how, but everything went terribly wrong. With a box mix! It turned out to be the most God-awful cake I'd ever seen. It was the definition of rubbery.

I can't remember baking anything from scratch until I got to cooking class in junior high. Still, it didn't pique my interest back then. It wasn't until I was finishing high school that the kitchen bug hit me. I've always loved food and decided to take it upon myself to level up our family's meals and desserts. So while my friends in high school were watching MTV I was watching the Food Network. I was reading cookbooks and recipe magazines while everyone else was obsessed with *Twilight*. My obsession didn't fade, so as I began college, feeling completely unsure about myself and my future, I started Handle the Heat in 2009 to chronicle my kitchen adventures and channel my creativity. By age twenty-three, I had written my first cookbook and graduated from culinary school. Today, more than ten years after my first post, that little blog has expanded beyond my wildest dreams and turned into my full-time business.

Even if it hadn't become my business, I know I'd be baking during every free moment I could find. For me it's the perfect blend of science and creativity. There are rules you have to color within, but in that space

Opposite: Captions left to right, top to bottom: My 1st birthday cake; beloved play kitchen; the last time I had fun doing dishes; cookie experiments in 2013; my first cookbook; realizing the joy of food at age 5; culinary school; lifelong sweet tooth; building my digital empire

Above: Captions left to right: When I discovered my love for chocolate, 2nd birthday cake; pure sugar bliss

you can explore and experiment. There's always something new to learn and improve. It rarely gets old, always feels therapeutic, and the sweet rewards at the end make all of the dirty dishes worth it. Not to mention the look of pure bliss on someone's face when they take a bite of your delicious creation.

My philosophy is that dessert should be an indulgence that's savored with every mouthwatering bite. That's why you won't see "healthy" recipes or alternatives in this book. Give me all of the real butter, flour, sugar, and cream! You'll also learn exactly how those ingredients work and why "healthy" substitutions and alternatives often can't perform the same function on a chemical level. Being equipped with even a simple understanding of the science of baking can change your kitchen game for life, which is why I'm so passionate about sharing it in a fun and easy way.

How to Use this Book

The first part of this book is jam-packed with my best baking tips and tricks, so don't skip it! The pages before the recipes in cookbooks are often overlooked, but this is where I share the bulk of my secrets that you won't want to miss.

Start with Smart Cookie, where I share the secrets to becoming a better baker instantly and get into the juicy stuff, including my best advice for making cookie dough step by step, the shocking importance of temperature in baking, and how to store cookies and cookie dough so you'll always be only minutes away from satisfying a cookie craving. In Baking Ingredients Explained, I dive into the anatomy of a cookie recipe to explain how baking ingredients actually work. I also share a basic cookie recipe that you can use as a base for creating your own recipes.

Then comes the fun part. In Cookie Customization, I take that base control recipe and show you the exact steps to transform it into the cookie of your dreams. Whether you want chewier, softer, taller, thicker, cakier, thinner, or crispier cookies, you can achieve exactly that with the tweaks shared here. In addition to sharing how to make those changes

happen, I'll explain why they work so you can create your own ultimate recipe. Each and every tweak is accompanied by a visual representation so you can *see* the science at work, which I think is the best and easiest way to learn. Science never looked so sweet!

In Cookie Troubleshooting, I detail everything imaginable to help you end your cookie baking frustrations. If your cookies ever come out wrong, chances are I've shared a picture of those bad cookies to help you identify and fix the problem. Banish failed cookies from your kitchen once and for all!

In the second half of the book, you'll find more than 50 cookie recipes. There are tons of variations on chocolate chip cookies that are not just fun and delicious, but also help to illustrate the secrets of cookie magic even further. There's Classic Cookies, which include my go-to recipes like Soft & Chewy Sugar Cookies and Snickerdoodles, and Fun Flavors, which showcases an array of color, texture, and tastes that will have your mouth watering. Of course, I had to dedicate an entire chapter to chocolate recipes and another to bar cookies, which hold a special place in my heart. Then to wrap things up, I share all of my holiday favorites to bake from Halloween to Christmas.

I hope this book will forever improve your cookie baking. I hope you love all of the recipes. As always, I love to see photos of your creations, so don't forget to snap some pictures and share with me online.

Happy baking!

PART I

Cookie Science

Become a Better Baker *Instantly*

Using this handbook is easy, but before you explore the world of cookie baking, it's important to read this chapter. It's loaded with useful information to help you understand the rest of the book and improve your baking skills forever. Skip it and the cookie monster will be after you!

One of the best pieces of advice I can give you is to never underestimate the fact that baking is truly a science. Just one small change while baking a recipe can hugely impact the final result. It's crazy and fascinating, but can make or break your success in the kitchen. Luckily, you don't need a chemistry degree to figure it all out. Here are my top four tips:

1. **Read the *entire* recipe before you start.** Have you ever gotten started on a recipe only to discover something unexpected like "chill overnight"? Reading the recipe entirely before starting will not only give you a smoother baking experience but also help you to feel more confident when you do enter the kitchen.

2. **Follow the recipe *exactly*.** Recipe developers spend countless hours experimenting and testing out methods to create the best recipe

possible. Skipping steps, making substitutions, or other changes not specified in the recipe may cause the results to be different than you hoped. On a related note, let me answer a question I am asked often: in cookie baking, "healthy" ingredient substitutions will never compete with the original. You will almost always sacrifice flavor or texture. If you are experienced in baking you can make educated changes with decent results but know that in doing so you are taking a risk.

3. ***Exactly* means paying attention to the sensory indicators given in the recipe.** Times given are estimates and how long something takes in your kitchen environment with your equipment will vary slightly. That's why it's absolutely critical to take note of the sensory indications, such as how a recipe should look, feel, and smell, first and foremost.

4. **Have fun! Even though baking is a science it's supposed to be *fun*.** Enjoy every step, no matter how much of a mess you make, because you will be rewarded with something delicious at the end. And if it's not delicious, well you learned a baking lesson you'll likely never forget!

EQUIPMENT

A baker's kitchen is nothing without the proper tools. You may think you have the right tools, but keep in mind they can make a surprising impact on the final product. Just take a look at the difference the kind of baking pan you use can make!

Baking Sheets Quality baking sheets are essential to baking good cookies. I love to use half sheet pans made from heavy-duty shiny aluminum, which resist warping. Aluminum is an excellent conductor of heat and will help your cookies bake more evenly. Insulated baking sheets will prevent your cookies from browning fully on the bottom. Conversely, dark nonstick bakeware can burn the bottoms of cookies.

BAKING SHEET COMPARISON CHART
T-FAL
Air Pan
WILTON
Non-Stick
WALMART
Budget Pan
Ceramic
Lined
VIKING
Unlined
Aluminum
NORDICWARE
Gold
Nonstick
OXO
T-FAL
Air Pan
WILTON
Non-Stick
WALMART
Budget Pan
Ceramic
Lined
VIKING
Unlined
Aluminum
NORDICWARE
Gold
Nonstick
OXO

Cooling Racks When you remove your cookies from the oven, they may look undercooked, but carryover cooking from residual heat will finish them perfectly. Cooling racks allow cookies to cool more quickly and evenly than they would if left on the pan, helping you to avoid too much carryover cooking.

Digital Kitchen Scale As you'll see in the measuring section, a kitchen scale is an indispensible tool for a baker. If you want to instantly improve your baking, stop using measuring cups and start weighing your ingredients with a scale, especially when it comes to flour.

Measuring Spoons and Cups Your set of measuring spoons should include ¼ teaspoon, ½ teaspoon, 1 teaspoon, and 1 tablespoon. A set of dry measuring cups should include ¼ cup, ⅓ cup, ½ cup, and 1 cup. Avoid using 2-cup dry measuring cups because they tend to compact ingredients for inaccurate measurements. Stainless steel measuring spoons and cups are most durable, won't stain, and are often dishwasher friendly. To measure liquids, use a glass measuring cup. I prefer the 2-cup size. Read the measurements at eye-level. We'll talk more about measuring later in this chapter!

Mixing Bowls Small, medium, and large mixing bowls are crucial in any baker's kitchen. Avoid plastic bowls that can retain odors, colors, and fat. Also be sure to have at least one microwave-safe bowl for quickly melting ingredients like butter and chocolate.

Parchment Paper Parchment paper is coated with silicone that makes it nonstick, allowing cookies to release easily when done baking. I prefer pre-cut sheets of parchment to silicone baking mats for three reasons. First, you don't have to clean anything extra. Second, silicone mats are so slick that cookies tend to spread more quickly and brown more intensely. Third, cookies can sometimes create condensation and "sweat" as they cool on silicone baking mats, resulting in slightly soggy bottoms.

zero
OXO
Digital Kitchen Scale
Liquid Measuring Cup
Measuring Cups
Measuring Spoons
1 TABLESPOON 15.0ml
1 TEA SPOON 5.0ml
1/2 TEA SPOON 2.5ml
1/4 TEA SPOON 1.25ml

Spring-loaded Scoops Spring-loaded scoops are perfect for quickly and easily forming balls of cookie dough so they all bake evenly. I use the following three sizes in this book:

Small:	1 tablespoon dough
Medium:	1½ tablespoons dough
Large:	3 tablespoons dough

Note that different brands of scoops may yield slightly different amounts of dough (even if they specify the same amount). That is why yields given in the recipes in this book should be considered approximations.

Spatulas A few long-handled silicone spatulas are essential. They're slightly flexible, heat resistant, and usually dishwasher safe (at least the silicone part). Make sure yours have a pointed edge so you can scrape down the nooks and crannies of your mixing bowl and paddle attachment.

Stand Mixer or Hand Mixer These small kitchen appliances can be used interchangeably and are a must when it comes to making cookie dough. I adore my KitchenAid 5-quart stand mixer for whipping up cookie dough in a snap.

Thermometer An oven thermometer is a necessity to make sure your oven is heating accurately. As you'll see in the coming chapters, even a small temperature variance can result in completely different cookies.

Whisks A couple of quality stainless steel wire whisks will eliminate lumps in ingredients like flour, brown sugar, and powdered sugar, and combine mixtures quickly. A small whisk is useful for making icing.

MEASURING *(the most important part of baking!)*

Measuring incorrectly can lead to kitchen flops, disappointments, misses, or complete fails. The problems in at least half of the "what went wrong?" questions I get asked by readers can be attributed to inaccurate measuring. (And if it's not incorrect measuring, it's often another accuracy issue.)

I'll say it again: the most foolproof path to baking success is to measure accurately. This will practically guarantee consistent results. I implore you to invest in a digital food scale if you don't already have one. It's a small investment to ensure consistent baking success. Weighing your ingredients is easy, fast, and clean. Plus, it's how the pros do it.

To use a digital kitchen scale, place your mixing bowl on the scale. Press the "zero" or "tare" button to take away the weight of the bowl. Add your ingredient until you achieve the weight called for in the recipe. You may need to give or take a few tablespoons to land directly on that number. Hit the tare button again to reset the weight to 0 before moving on to the next ingredient. It's that easy!

TIP: *Keep a list of the weights of your most commonly used mixing bowls, such as your stand mixer bowl, handy on your phone or in your kitchen so you can continue measuring accurately even if you've forgotten to tare.*

Note that different ingredients have different densities. This means that 1 cup of every ingredient will not weigh the same. Think about it: 1 cup of feathers would not weigh the same as 1 cup of sand, right? See the Ingredients Measuring Guide on page 209 for a list of weights of common baking ingredients, some of which are also included below. Weight measurements are provided in the recipes in this book.

If you don't have a scale and don't plan on using one, I've included tips for measuring by volume with dry and liquid measuring cups below (though I really wish you'd use a scale!).

Liquid vs. Dry Measuring Cups

The general rule is, if you can pour it use a liquid measuring cup (oil, honey, maple syrup, etc.). If you can smooth the top, use a dry measuring cup (peanut butter, sour cream).

Measuring Spoons I prefer to use measuring spoons to weigh out anything that is a tablespoon or smaller. I find that many home use digital kitchen scales simply aren't sensitive enough to accurately weigh such small measurements. I also think it's quicker and easier than a scale when working with small amounts. You'll see this reflected in the recipe measurements provided throughout the book.

Flour Unfortunately, flour can be very difficult to measure by volume (using measuring cups). It is arguably the easiest ingredient to mismeasure, and a mismeasured cup of flour can ruin your baking project. When it comes to measuring flour, a digital scale is your best friend, but if you do use measuring cups, here are some tips. Scooping your measuring cup directly into your container of flour can pack the flour in, causing your measurement to be too dense. In fact, this method can lead a cup of flour to weigh almost 2 ounces more than other methods! This can make a huge difference in the composition of your baked goods. If you've ever had cookies not spread in the oven or turn dry or crumbly, those are just some examples of what too much flour can do in baking.

Instead, use the "spoon and level" method

Fluff up your container of flour. Spoon the flour into your measuring cup, then scrape off the excess with a straight edge. A flour scoop is the best tool for this. This will get you about 4.5 ounces or 127 grams of all-purpose flour per cup.

Note that different kinds of flour have slightly different weights. The table below shows the standard weights I've used throughout this book. Different flour brands have different weights, too, and some cookbooks may use different approximations for ingredients. Follow the author's weight measurements or conversion guide for the best results.

All-purpose flour:	1 cup = 4.5 ounces = 127 grams
Bread flour:	1 cup = 4.5 ounces = 127 grams
Cake flour:	1 cup = 4 ounces = 113 grams
Whole wheat flour:	1 cup = 4.5 ounces = 127 grams

Baking Powder and Baking Soda

Shake up the container of leavener slightly, then use a measuring spoon to lightly scoop a mound. Use a flat edge to scrape off the excess.

Granulated Sugar

Measuring granulated sugar is a little simpler than flour. Use your measuring cup as a scoop to dip into the container then use a flat edge to scrape off any excess.

1 cup = 7.05 ounces = 200 grams

Brown Sugar

Pay attention to the measurement direction written in the recipe, which will usually say "brown sugar, lightly packed." This is basically the opposite of flour measuring and means you gently pack the brown sugar into the measuring cup until it reaches the brim. That is how I call for brown sugar in this cookbook. Make sure to break any large clumps before measuring.

1 cup packed light or dark brown sugar = 7.05 ounces = 200 grams

Powdered Sugar Also called confectioners' sugar or icing sugar, this stuff can make a huge mess when you measure it. Spoon the sugar into your measuring cup then use a straight edge to scrape off any excess.

1 cup powdered sugar = 4.4 ounces = 125 grams

It often needs to be sifted before being added to recipes since it can be lumpy. Make sure you understand the order of sifting and measuring:

1 cup powdered sugar, sifted = sift *after* measuring

1 cup sifted powdered sugar = sifted *before* measuring
(I avoid calling for this because it makes a mess!)

Liquid Sweeteners If a recipe calls for oil and a liquid sweetener, measure the oil first to grease the measuring cup. You can also spray nonstick cooking spray inside the measuring cup before measuring sticky ingredients.

Butter There are so many forms of measurement used for butter in recipes that it can be absolutely confusing. I call for sticks or tablespoons and grams. I know this is still confusing for some, so here is a super useful equivalent for butter measurements.

1 stick = 8 tablespoons = ½ cup = 4 ounces = 113 grams

Cookie 101 (don't skip this!)

HOW TO MAKE THE BEST DROP COOKIES, STEP BY STEP

Most of the recipes in this book are for drop-style cookies. This simply means that you drop balls of cookie dough on a baking sheet. No rolling, slicing, or cookie cutting. They are simpler and easier than most other cookies and lend themselves to customization, tweaking, and experimenting. I know you may be tempted to skip this section. If you've made one drop-style cookie recipe, haven't you made them all?

It's true. The steps are pretty much the same in every recipe. However, there are small details in each of those steps that, when mastered, can make the difference between good and consistently great cookies. These are the differences cookie pros know, so listen up!

1. **Preheating** Preheat your oven at least 15 minutes before baking. See my Oven 101 tips (page 34) and baking pan recommendations (page 20).

2. **Measuring** Measure your dry ingredients accurately. I've said it before, but this is best done with a kitchen scale. Whisk them together to ensure the mixture is clump-free and the leaveners and salt are evenly distributed.

3. **Creaming** Use an electric mixer on medium high speed to beat the cool room temperature butter and any sugar called for in the recipe. This creaming process blends the ingredients together, and the sugar crystals hitting against the butter create tiny pockets of air that help to leaven the dough so it's not too dense. For cookies, this should only take about 2 to 3 minutes. You're looking for the mixture to be smooth, pale in color, and fluffy in texture (as opposed to sandy and gritty after the first minute of beating). If you're making a cake, you'll likely beat for a little longer. That's because cakes need more air to develop their tall,

soft, light, and delicate structure. If you cream too long when making cookies, the cookies may collapse upon cooling. If your butter is too warm, it won't incorporate any air and will also collapse your cookies. 65–67°F is the perfect cool room temperature butter.

4. **Mixing** Scrape everything down as you go! This includes the sides of the bowl, the *bottom* of the bowl, and your paddle attachment. Do this even if you have an attachment that scrapes as it turns. For perfectly formed cookie dough, you'll want to scrape down your mixture at least 3 times during the entire process, both during the creaming process and after you add the egg. Unincorporated pockets of butter create those random exploded looking cookies, or simply cookies that are uneven and unappetizing (you know the ones that kids fight over not getting).
   - Add the eggs, one at a time. I like to crack my eggs into a small separate bowl just in case a shell ends up in the mix. Allow each egg to completely incorporate into the mixture before adding the next one. Eggs incorporate better at room temperature.
   - Slowly and gradually add the dry ingredient mixture so you don't end up with flour everywhere. Mix until just combined.
   - Slowly mix in any add-ins like chocolate chips, candy, or nuts. The more you mix the dough after the flour is added, the more gluten will develop to create a chewier or denser texture. Sometimes this is desired, other times it's not. For a more delicate texture, mix the add-ins by hand with a rubber spatula.

5. **Shaping** Use a spring-loaded scoop to make quick work of shaping the dough into even balls. If you want a smoother looking cookie, roll the balls of dough between the palms of your hands before placing them on the baking sheet. Some recipes call for rolling the dough, and some simply call for dropping the dough, depending on how they look and bake up best.

6. **Baking** Place the pan in your properly heated oven and set your timer for the low end of the time given in the recipe. Every oven heats differently, every pan conducts heat differently, and every kitchen environment is slightly different. Take special note of the sensory indications given in the recipe and follow those first. Check on your cookies and if they look *almost* done but still slightly moist in the center, remove them from the oven. They will continue to bake from the residual heat.

7. **Cooling** Allow to cool for as long as the recipe specifies on the baking sheets before transferring to cooling racks to cool completely.

> **TIP:** *If you're making a recipe you've never made before, I suggest baking off just a few cookies to begin with and seeing how they turn out. From there, you can add more flour or chill the dough if they come out thinner than you desire. You can adjust the baking time or temperature. You can scoop smaller or bigger sizes, and so on.*

OVEN 101

Every oven heats differently. Even where you place your cookies in the oven can have a surprising effect on the final result! In this section, I'll help you to unlock the keys to success when it comes to your oven.

Temperature An oven thermometer is a necessity to make sure your oven is heating accurately. Besides a kitchen scale, it's the best money you can spend for your general baking! Many home ovens are off by 15 degrees, some by even 25 degrees or more! I've never found a home oven that was 100 percent accurate. In fact, my new oven often tells me it's preheated to the temperature I specified when it's actually at least 20 degrees cooler. It may not seem like a big difference, but baking at the wrong temperature can significantly change your final product. Take a look:

To test your own oven's accuracy, follow the steps below. You may be shocked by the results.

1. Place your oven thermometer so it's in the center of the middle oven rack (where you'd place anything to bake).

2. Preheat to 350°F. Write down the temperature when the oven beeps to say it's preheated. Check again in 10 minutes and write down that temperature. Do you need to wait longer for the oven to properly preheat moving forward? This is the case with most ovens.

3. Now raise the temperature to 425°F. Write down the temperature when the oven beeps to say it's heated. Check again in 10 minutes and write down that temperature.

4. Note any discrepancies and adjust your oven temperature and preheat time accordingly.

Baking Time A few minutes can make a big difference in how your cookies turn out. Always set a timer and experiment with your oven and how well baked you prefer your cookies to be to get the best results.

Placement The position of your oven rack can also have a surprising impact on your cookies. Some recipes will specifically tell you where to position your oven rack, but most of the time it should be in the middle. Why? This is where the heat will be most even. If you bake your cookies (or anything) on the top rack, there won't be as much browning. On the bottom rack, there will likely be too much browning.

Overcrowding The same effect can occur when you're baking multiple dishes at once. The other baking pans can block the heat from moving around freely and screw up the way the product bakes and browns. If you can, try to bake one batch of anything at a time instead of doing multiple pans together. If you can't, rotate the pans halfway through baking. You may need to rotate your pans if your oven has noticeable hot spots as well.

PLACEMENT COMPARISON CHART

Top Rack

Middle Rack

Bottom Rack

Convection Fan Ovens Convection ovens have a fan that circulates the heat more quickly, evenly, and efficiently than conventional ovens. A few tips:

- Never overcrowd a convection oven, the air can't blow around.
- Make the proper adjustments: Drop the temperature 25°F from what is specified in the recipe. Some ovens with a convection setting will adjust the temperature automatically (check with your oven manufacturer). Check for doneness two-thirds or three-quarters of the way through the recommended baking time.

Adjusted

PICTURE-PERFECT COOKIES

We truly eat with our eyes, so taking a few extra moments to make your cookies beautiful is worth the effort!

1. Prep Your Dough Before you even shape your dough, really make sure you've scraped down the sides and bottom of the bowl, your blade attachment, and your spatula. Any unincorporated pockets of butter will create misshapen splattered-looking cookies.

2. Use a Scoop! The best tip for making picture-perfect cookies is to use a spring-loaded scoop to create precisely uniform balls of dough.

3. Stop, Drop, and Roll Roll the balls between your palms to smooth any lumps and bumps. Unless, of course, you desire a more craggy and uneven appearance, which works better for some recipes.

4. Garnish If you're making a cookie with mix-ins such as chocolate chips, press a few on top of the ball of dough. As the cookie bakes and spreads, the chocolate chips will spread apart and look absolutely perfect!

5. What If My Cookies Aren't Perfectly Round? If you followed the steps above and your cookies still aren't nice neat circles, not to worry. As soon as your cookies come out of the oven, use a spoon or round cookie cutter to press the uneven hot cookie edges back into a circular shape.

COOKIE STORAGE

Baked Cookies

In general, cooled cookies can be stored in an airtight container at room temperature for 3 to 5 days, depending on the recipe. Cookie cutter recipes tend to keep longer. To keep the cookies soft, add an apple wedge, tortilla, or piece of bread to the container. To reheat them, place in an oven heated to 350°F for 3 to 5 minutes, or until warmed through.

Cookie Dough

I prefer to refrigerate or freeze my dough and bake cookies as I want them, because nothing beats fresh, still-warm cookies. Cookie dough can be stored in the fridge, covered, for up to 3 days. Let sit at room temperature until warm enough to scoop. Balls of cookie dough can also be placed on a cookie sheet and frozen. Once frozen, transfer the balls to an airtight container and store in the freezer for up to 6 weeks. Bake from frozen, dropping the oven temperature by 25°F and adding an additional few minutes to the cooking time. Or, bring dough to defrost at room temperature and bake as directed by the recipe.

2 CHAPTER | Baking Ingredients EXPLAINED

Don't you wish you had spent tenth grade science class dissecting cookies? A solid understanding of the anatomy of a cookie and how all of the ingredients work together will help you tremendously in the kitchen.

The following is much more than a list of common cookie baking ingredients. I've started by providing detailed insights into the most important and common baking ingredients. These ingredients make up the foundation of most baking techniques and recipes and it's crucial to understand how they work. This is the first step in understanding how and why your cookies turn out the way they do, and how to change them to get your desired result.

TIP: *As you'll see over the coming pages, each ingredient performs a very specific chemical function. Substituting ingredients often changes the integrity of the chemistry of a recipe. I highly recommend baking all of the recipes in this book exactly as they are written, at least the first time you try one. Then you can use the guidance in the customization section on page 67 to tweak them.*

Flour

Flour is a huge component of any standard cookie recipe. It is not only tremendously important to accurately measure the flour, but also to understand that different types of flour products and even different brands of flour can greatly affect the finished cookie.

HOW FLOUR WORKS IN BAKING

1. **Builds Structure** Possibly the most important function flour accomplishes in baked goods is building structure. It's actually one of two main ingredients that build structure, the other being eggs. The amount and type of flour you use will have a significant impact on the shape and texture of your cookies. Gluten and starch are the main structure building components in flour. Generally, gluten is more important in unbaked dough while starch is more important in the actual baking process.

What Is Gluten? Let's talk about how gluten actually works, because it's really important but generally misunderstood or overlooked. Gluten can be described as a network of strong, flexible webs that act as the backbone of many baked goods. Gluten only forms when the proteins in flour combine with water and are physically mixed or kneaded. The higher the protein content in a type of flour, the more gluten will form into that strong web when water is added and mixed. Take a look at the chart to see how different flours have different amounts of protein. (To calculate the protein content in any flour, divide the grams of protein per serving by the total grams per serving listed in the nutrition facts label.)

Protein Content of Flour

Flour Type	Percent Protein
Bread flour	12–15%
All-purpose flour	9–12%
King Arthur all-purpose flour	11.7%
Gold Medal and Pillsbury all-purpose flour	10.5%
Pastry flour	9%
Cake flour	6–8%

So why does the protein content matter? Well, when the protein in flour is combined with liquid and mixed, it creates the gluten that gives structure to baked goods. Bread, for example, needs lots of structure to rise tall and sturdy. This is why bread flour has the most protein. Delicate and tender cakes require very little gluten structure, which is why cake flour has the least protein. In cookie baking, knowing the percent of protein in your flour can help you figure out why your cookies come out the way they do. We'll look at how bread flour and cake flour impact cookies, complete with visuals, ahead and in the Cookie Customization chapter on page 67.

2. **Absorbs Liquid** Flour is considered a "drier," meaning that it absorbs moisture and oil and helps bind ingredients together. As cookie dough sits, for example during a 24-hour chilling period, the flour will continue to absorb moisture from the dough.

3. **Contributes Color, Flavor, and Nutritional Value** The nutritional value will depend on the type of flour used.

TYPES OF FLOUR

Cake Flour Besides having the lowest level of protein content, cake flour is also finely milled from soft wheat from the heart of the wheat endosperm. This gives cake flour that characteristic fine texture. Cake flour is typically bleached with both chlorine and benzoyl peroxide, which gives it that stark white color and a distinct flavor. Bleaching with chlorine actually weakens the gluten and increases the flour's ability to soak up more water and oils, producing thicker, stiffer batter and dough. These unique characteristics are why it's basically impossible to recreate cake flour's unique properties at home with DIY "cake flour" made from sifting all-purpose flour and cornstarch. Products made with cake flour will have a very fine, light, and delicate cake-like crumb and pale color with little browning. Take a look:

All-Purpose Flour

All-Purpose Flour This falls in the middle of the protein content chart, but the exact percentage of protein will depend on the brand you use and what varieties of wheat they use to manufacture their flour.

Bleached vs. Unbleached Foods made with bleached flour tend to have a softer texture, more volume, and a lighter color than those made with unbleached flour. Bleached flour also soaks up more moisture, which can help make slightly thicker cookies. For this book, all recipes were tested using Gold Medal Blue Label Bleached all-purpose flour. Its blend of red and white wheat and medium protein content make it my first choice for truly "all-purpose" baking.

Bread Flour

Milled from hard wheat, this high-protein flour forms good-quality gluten networks. You can see the differences in the comparisons below.

All-Purpose Flour

Bread flour can also yield cookies that are thicker and chewier than their all-purpose flour counterparts. That's why I love to use half bread flour and half all-purpose flour in my Ultimate Chewy Chocolate Chip Cookie recipe (page 96).

Sugar

Sugar most obviously lends sweetness to a recipe, but it also seriously impacts a cookie's texture and color in ways most people never realize.

HOW SUGAR WORKS IN BAKING

1. **Sweetens** First and most obviously, sugar sweetens the flavor of any recipe.

2. **Moistens and Tenderizes** If you've ever made candy or caramel, you know that sugar liquefies when heated. Sugar actually interferes with gluten formation, protein coagulation, and starch gelatinization. This is basically a complicated way of saying that sugar creates a tender texture.

TIP: *The term hygroscopic refers to the phenomenon of attracting and holding water molecules from the surrounding environment. All sugar attracts water, which prevents that water from being used to form tough strands of gluten. This is what helps create that tender and moist texture. Some sugar is more hygroscopic than other sugars. For example, brown sugar is more hygroscopic than granulated sugar. That means cookies made with brown sugar will be slightly more tender and moist, whereas cookies made with granulated sugar will be crisper and spread out thinner because it doesn't absorb as much water. This water-pulling nature of sugar also helps prevent foods from going stale, acting as a preservative to extend shelf life. It's why cookies made with more sugar are softer and stay fresher longer.*

3. **Leavens** Next, sugar assists in leavening, or helping baked goods lift and rise for a taller shape and lighter texture. When you cream butter and dry sugar together, the sugar drills tiny holes into the butter which expand and bubble when exposed to the heat of the oven. Learn more about the importance of the creaming process on page 31.

4. **Browns and Caramelizes** Most sweeteners also contribute a brown color and pleasant caramelized flavor through the processes of caramelization and Maillard browning. Basically, they help to form that golden brown crust that is so delicious.

See . . . I wasn't kidding when I said sugar does a lot more than create a sweet taste!

TYPES OF SUGAR

Granulated Sugar

This is also called white sugar, and is commonly made from sugarcane or sugar beets.

Brown Sugar

Brown sugar is made from a combination of granulated sugar and a small amount of molasses, a viscous liquid formed as a by-product of sugar production. The molasses helps to create a more complex butterscotch sweet flavor and draws in more moisture. Unlike granulated sugar, brown sugar is acidic and will react more with any baking soda in a recipe. Dark brown sugar simply has more molasses than light brown sugar.

Granulated Sugar vs. Brown Sugar Let's take a peek at how granulated sugar and brown sugar look when used in cookies. Generally, the granulated sugar cookies will spread out flatter and wider, while cookies made with brown sugar will be slightly thicker.

Granulated Sugar

Brown Sugar

DIY Brown Sugar

You can make your own brown sugar by combining granulated sugar with molasses.

1 cup (200 grams) granulated sugar

1 tablespoon unsulphured molasses for light brown sugar *or* 2 to 3 tablespoons for dark brown sugar

In a large bowl, use an electric mixer to combine the sugar and molasses until completely incorporated. Use or store in an airtight container. Use a brown sugar saver to keep it from hardening. If the sugar does become hard, you can still add the soaked brown sugar saver to soften it. You can also add a slice of bread for a few hours, which will soften it again.

Powdered Sugar Also called confectioners' sugar or icing sugar, powdered sugar is simply granulated sugar that's been pulverized into a fine powder. Some labels will actually specify how finely ground the sugar is. If possible, use 10x ground powdered sugar for icing and frosting recipes. Save 6x powdered sugar for when you want to dust or coat cookies with powdered sugar and don't want the powder to melt and liquefy. Powdered sugar also typically contains a small amount of cornstarch, which absorbs moisture and helps prevent caking. Even so, it's always a smart idea to sift powdered sugar to remove any lumps before using.

Liquid Sweeteners Also sometimes called invert syrup, this includes corn syrup, maple syrup, honey, and molasses. Generally, liquid sweeteners will keep baked goods soft and moist for longer.

Molasses Always use unsulphured molasses in baking. Avoid using blackstrap molasses, which is extremely bitter and dark in color.

Honey A natural invert syrup, honey is prized for its unique flavor and ability to brown easily and keep baked goods and icings soft and moist.

Maple Syrup Used for its unique and very sweet aroma, only pure maple syrup should be used in baking (not imitation maple-flavored pancake syrup). Darker colored syrups are strong in flavor, low in grade, and lower in price. For an all-purpose maple syrup, go for Grade A Medium Amber in the US or No. 1 Light in Canada.

In general, liquid sweeteners create a cakier texture due to the extra moisture they contribute. You'll see in a few recipes I use a spoonful of honey or maple syrup for this exact reason. Here are some examples:

Fat

In this book I use the word "fat" as a general term encompassing products including oil, butter, and shortening.

WHAT FAT DOES IN BAKING

1. Tenderizes Fats lubricate starches and proteins in doughs and batters, preventing them from hydrating and forming gluten structures. Think of baked goods that contain no fat—like a French baguette. They're chewy, dry, and crusty. Tender products made with fat, on the other hand, are generally easy to squeeze, break, crumble, and chew.

2. Moistens More accurately, fats create the *sensation* of moistness, especially ones that are liquid at room temperature. Unlike water, fat can't be absorbed by starches or proteins, or held onto by sugar, so with the right fat content, a baked good can feel wonderfully moist without actually containing any water.

3. Leavens Fats can assist in leavening baked goods in a few different ways. Leavening occurs when we beat a fat like butter with sugar, creating lots of tiny air bubbles which expand when exposed to heat. Layers of fat in laminated dough, such as croissant dough, also help with leavening: when heat from the oven hits the water in the butter, pockets of steam form and lift the dough to create those flaky layers.

4. Contributes Flavor Butter is often used for its unparalleled flavor, but all fats add a certain level of richness and help to round out and enhance other flavors in the mix. In fact, some flavor compounds are fat soluble, meaning they are best tasted when there's fat in the mix.

5. Assists in Browning The milk solids in butter can also assist in browning via the Maillard reaction, which creates that beautiful brown crust and complex flavor profile (think of brown butter!).

6. Other Functions of Fat It also prevents baked goods from going stale, conducts heat for even cooking, prevents sticking, and increases spread in cookies.

TYPES OF FAT

Butter

Made from churning cream, butter is probably the most commonly used form of fat in baking cookies. That's because butter has a flavor and mouth feel that no other fat can compete with. That "melt-in-your mouth" sensation is thanks to butter having a melting temperature around body temperature. Butter is one of the most crucial elements of any cookie dough. As you'll see in the coming chapters, its form can greatly influence the final cookie. Perfect room temperature butter for cookie baking should:

- Give slightly when pressed with your finger but still hold its shape
- Be flexible without breaking or cracking
- Be at a cool room temperature of about 65–67°F

It's better for the butter to be too cool than too warm. When butter is the perfect temperature it will hold the optimal amount of air from the creaming process to create perfectly thick cookies. See the comparison below:

If you don't have time to let butter sit out to come to room temperature, here are some quick ways to warm it.

- **Microwave:** This is the fastest method but also the trickiest because you can easily overheat the butter, which often leads to flat and greasy cookies. Place stick(s) of butter on a microwave-safe plate. Microwave for 4 to 5 seconds, then turn the stick on its side. Continue microwaving and turning the butter until all four sides have been warmed or until the butter reaches a cool room temperature.
- **Cube:** Cut the butter into small cubes and let them sit until they reach a cool room temperature.

- **Grate:** This works best with frozen butter. Use a box grater to grate the butter into a bowl and let it sit until it has softened to a cool room temperature

North American vs. European Butter North American butter must contain at least 80 percent butterfat. The remaining 20 percent is made of water, milk solids like proteins and sugar (lactose), and salt, if added. European-style butter has slightly more butterfat, a minimum of 82 percent, but often 86 percent or more. Butter with more butterfat typically has a smoother, creamier mouth feel so it's particularly delicious when spread on bread. The recipes in this book were tested with North American–style butter.

Salted vs. Unsalted Butter I'm a strong proponent of using unsalted butter in all baking, so I always have some on hand in my fridge or freezer. Since there is no industry standard for how much salt is in a pound of salted butter, it's impossible to be accurate about the total salt content of a recipe. In fact, some brands have twice as much salt as others! If you do need to use salted butter, omit half or all of the salt called for in the recipe.

Margarine This is a butter replacement, or imitation butter. It's made up of oil, saturated fat, and milk ingredients to replicate the general makeup of butter. Though it is much cheaper than real butter, it doesn't actually taste or feel like butter so I don't use it in my baking.

Shortening Unlike butter, shortening is 100 percent fat and contains no water. That's why the shortening product packaging will tell you to add water to a recipe if you're replacing the butter with shortening.

Generally 1 stick (113 grams) butter = ½ cup shortening + 1 tablespoon water

Shortening is unique in that about 10 percent of its volume is air, specifically nitrogen, which can be used to leaven foods like cakes. It's slightly easier

Shortening *Continued*

to work with in some recipes because its melting temperature is higher than butter, at about 110–120°F (butter melts at approximately 90°F). This can make it easier to work with in frosting, because it won't melt as easily as butter. However, this also means it doesn't have that "melt-in-your-mouth" feel and can leave a layer of greasy film behind on the palate.

Butter vs. Shortening In cookies, shortening creates a lovely thicker texture but lacks the wonderful flavor of butter. Let's take a look at how the two stack up:

If you want to use shortening in your cookie baking, I recommend using half shortening and half butter so you can get the best of both.

Oil

100 percent fat, oil has no proteins, solids, water, or air. The most commonly used oil in the baker's kitchen is vegetable oil, which is often made from soybeans or cottonseed. Oil is the only common fat that doesn't contribute to leavening in baked goods, since it can't trap air or water. That's why oil is used most often in quick breads and muffins, which are leavened by a higher amount of baking powder and baking soda. The only exception is coconut oil, which is solid at room temperature. If you want the coconut taste, use unrefined virgin coconut oil. If you want a neutral taste, use refined coconut oil. Measure coconut oil when it's creamy and solid, around 70°F.

Eggs

WHAT EGGS DO IN BAKING

1. Provide Structure The most important function they serve is forming structure in your favorite baked goods. Coagulated proteins in both egg whites and yolks serve a unique structural role as "tougheners." The fats and emulsifiers in the yolk also work as tenderizers. Eggs are especially important for providing structure for custards, meringues, and cakes such as angel food cake. They don't need to work quite as hard in most cookie recipes.

2. Yolks Contribute Color and Flavor One of my favorite quick tips for creating a chewier cookie is to add an extra egg yolk to the dough! The fat and little bit of extra protein help create the wonderful texture.

3. Add Nutritional Value

4. Prevent Staling Eggs can do many other things in other kinds of recipes, but for our cookie concerns, the last important function they can serve is to maintain freshness. Eggs contain an all-natural emulsifier called lecithin that is concentrated in the yolk, which essentially helps retain moisture and prevent staling.

EGG WHITES VS. EGG YOLKS

Egg whites contain lots of moisture, a little more than half the protein of the egg, and zero fat (and therefore little flavor). Egg yolks contain a little less than half the protein of the whole egg, less water, and all of the fat of the egg, so they offer lots of flavor. They also have emulsifying properties that can bring batters together fast. Generally, if you replace a whole egg with just yolks, the texture will be more tender and rich. If you replace a whole egg with just whites, the texture will be drier and leaner, even cakier.

In these side-by-side examples, the cookie on the left was made with an extra egg white, the center was the control with whole eggs, and the cookie on the right was made with an extra egg yolk.

EGG CLASSIFICATIONS

Brown eggs and white eggs are virtually the same. However, egg sizes can make a world of difference. Most recipes use large eggs, but you should use whatever size your recipe calls for. As you can see in the tables below, the various sizes of eggs vary widely in mass, and those differences can completely change the ratios and chemistry of the recipe you're making. If no size is called for, you can generally assume that large eggs will work. In the US, size classifications represent the minimum weight for the entire dozen that is set by the USDA, so individual eggs will vary in weight. The charts below show average weights.

Egg Weight Minimums by Size

Labeled size	US and Canada	EU
Small	42 grams	
Medium	49 grams	53 grams
Large	56 grams	63 grams
Very large or extra large	63 grams	73 grams
Jumbo	70 grams	

Large Egg Weight Averages

Type of egg	US and Canada
Egg in shell	56 grams
Egg out of shell	50 grams
Egg white	30 grams
Egg yolk	18.6 grams

EGG SAFETY

Eggs should be stored in the back of the fridge. The USDA recommends that eggs should be cooked to 160°F to kill off any potentially dangerous bacteria like salmonella.

To test eggs for freshness:

- Place an egg in a bowl of water.
- If the egg lays on its side at the bottom, it is still quite fresh.
- If the egg stands upright on the bottom, it is still fine to eat, but should be eaten very soon, or hard-boiled.
- If the egg floats to the top, it's not good for eating and should be thrown away.

Leaveners

Leavening agents, or leaveners, cause baked goods to rise. They provide lightness and volume, making foods more tender and easier to digest.

TYPES OF LEAVENERS

Leavening Gases Leavening gases like air and carbon dioxide work to leaven your favorite baked goods by creating little bubbles that expand when exposed to the

Levening Gasses
Continued

heat of the oven. If you've ever under-mixed a batter, you may have experienced a flat and coarse final product because there wasn't enough air to expand and leaven. If you've ever overmixed a batter, you may have experienced a product that collapsed after baking because there was more air incorporated than the product could hold onto. When chemical leaveners are activated, little bubbles of carbon dioxide become trapped in the dough and expand when heated. Something similar occurs when the heat from the oven hits water in butter and turns into steam. This is how leavening gases work, and why it's important to follow the recipe instructions like, "whip," "fold," "cream," or "knead" carefully.

Chemical Leaveners

Baking powder and baking soda are both chemical leaveners that work to create light textures in baked goods—but only when they're fresh and accurately measured. Although baking powder actually contains baking soda, the two leaveners are very different. Baking powder and baking soda are not interchangeable.

Baking soda is a natural alkaline ingredient activated by liquid and acid present in the batter, dough, or mixture. Common acidic baking ingredients include buttermilk, sour cream, and yogurt; fruits and fruit juices; vinegar; most syrups, including honey and molasses; brown sugar; and natural cocoa powder (but not Dutch-process) and unsweetened chocolate. There must be some acidic ingredient in the recipe for baking soda to function. Baking soda begins to leaven as soon as it touches liquid, so if you wait too long before baking you may notice a decrease in leavening effect. If you use too much baking soda, you may taste an unpleasant metallic flavor in your food.

Since baking soda must be fresh to work properly, it's important to switch out your container before the expiration date. However, baking soda can lose its effectiveness even before that date.

To test baking soda for freshness, place ¼ teaspoon baking soda in a bowl and pour 1 teaspoon distilled vinegar on top. If the baking soda immediately bubbles violently, it is fresh. If nothing happens, throw away the baking soda and buy a new package.

Chemical Leaveners *Continued*

Baking powder is a combination of baking soda, acid, and cornstarch. Most baking powder available in the US is double acting, meaning its first reaction occurs when combined with liquid to help aerate the batter or dough and a second, slower reaction occurs when heated in the oven. Unlike baking soda, baking powder doesn't require additional acid to activate, only moisture. Baking powder batters can be made ahead of time due to their double-acting property.

Also unlike baking soda, baking powder contains multiple ingredients. This means different brands have different proportions of these ingredients and can positively or negatively affect how thick your cookies bake up. If you find your cookies are too cakey or too thin with no obvious explanation, try switching to a different brand of baking powder. I recommend using Argo, Bob's Red Mill, Calumet, or Clabber Girl.

To test baking powder for freshness, place 1 teaspoon baking powder in a bowl with 1 cup hot water from the tap. If it bubbles up, the baking powder is fresh. If nothing happens, throw the baking powder away and buy a new container.

Baking Soda vs. Baking Powder One is not better than the other, they're simply different! Baking soda elevates pH levels more than baking powder. This results in a beautiful browned color and increases spread in cookies by weakening the gluten structure. Baking powder can create lift and thickness in cookies since it's double acting. More specifically, the heat of the oven helps activate its leavening bubbles again as the dough cooks and sets before those bubbles can burst.

It's important to understand that baking soda is four times stronger than baking powder. This means 1 teaspoon of baking powder will raise a cup of flour, whereas only a ¼ teaspoon of baking soda is needed to produce the same effect.

Some recipes call for both baking soda and baking powder in order to have the highest effect of acid neutralizing and leavening powers. This works especially well for acidic dough that needs to be stored overnight.

Other Baking Ingredients

CHIPS AND MIX-INS

Anything from chocolate chips to peanut butter chips, butterscotch chips, caramel bits, nuts, candy, or whatever else you can fathom can be easily added to cookie dough. You can get creative here as long as whatever you swap in is similar in size and shape to the original mix-in so your balls of dough stay cohesive.

CHOCOLATE

Unsweetened

Unsweetened chocolate is 99 percent pure chocolate liquor or cocoa, with no sugar added. Also called baking chocolate, this is equal parts chocolate solids and cocoa butter.

Bittersweet and Semisweet

Bittersweet chocolate is, as the name implies, sweeter than unsweetened, but darker and more bitter than semisweet. There are no regulations that distinguish bittersweet from semisweet, both simply must contain at least 35 percent pure chocolate. Look at the packaging to determine the percentage of your chocolate and give it a taste test if you're unsure.

Milk

Milk chocolate must contain at least 10 to 15 percent cacao and is combined with dry milk powder, so it's significantly sweeter with a less intense chocolate flavor than even semisweet.

White

Real white chocolate should contain cocoa butter as the main fat, but does not contain any chocolate solids. Its main ingredients are cocoa butter (20 percent minimum), dry milk powder (14 percent), sugar (55 percent maximum), vanilla, and soy lecithin. High quality white chocolate should be creamy in color.

Couverture Couverture is ultra-high-quality chocolate usually used by pastry chefs. It has more cocoa butter added during manufacturing to make it ultrasmooth and easy to melt and dip.

Coating Chocolate Also called compound chocolate, coating chocolate is used in home candy making. It is not real chocolate, because the cocoa butter has been replaced by other fats. It comes in various colors and doesn't require tempering to hold its formed shape after being melted.

Chocolate Chips Available in dark, milk, and white chocolate, many chips on the market are actually imitation chocolate that contains no cocoa butter. In these varieties, the cocoa butter has been replaced with hydrogenated oil so that the chips hold their shape and are cheap to manufacture. Other stabilizers and additives are also used to help them keep their shape even after being melted. This is perfect for chocolate chip cookies. But when baking with a recipe that calls for melted chocolate, it's best to use freshly chopped baking chocolate, not chocolate chips, to ensure it melts down smoothly.

COCOA POWDER

The recipes in this book call for either natural unsweetened cocoa powder, often labeled simply "cocoa powder," or Dutch-process unsweetened cocoa powder.

Natural Cocoa Powder Natural cocoa is more typical in American recipes and supermarkets. Due to the fact that natural cocoa powder is highly acidic, it is often paired with baking soda as a leavener.

Dutch-process Cocoa Powder Dutch-process, which is more common in Europe, is treated with alkali to neutralize its acidity, soften its flavor, and change its color. It is therefore only slightly acidic with a more mellow flavor and rich brown color. Conversely to natural cocoa, Dutch-process cocoa is typically paired with baking powder as a leavener, since the acidity has been neutralized.

Dutch-process cocoa powder won't react much with baking soda unless there is additional acid in the recipe. That's why you should stick to the type of cocoa powder called for in the recipe. Dutch-process cocoa powder is more difficult to find in regular supermarkets, but you can usually purchase it at specialty and gourmet food stores or online.

Fat In Cocoa Powder

What's surprisingly important when choosing a cocoa powder to bake with, regardless of its type, is how much fat content it has. That fat content comes from the cocoa butter. In the United States, the FDA requires a minimum of 10 percent cocoa butter in cocoa powder, but some brands contain more than double that amount. More fat generally creates a richer chocolate flavor and a moister, more tender texture. You can look up the fat content online, or estimate it from the nutrition facts. Compare the amount of fat in the nutrition facts among different brands when shopping.

CREAM CHEESE

Cream cheese imparts a rich tangy flavor and soft texture to cookie recipes.

ESPRESSO POWDER

A small amount of espresso powder can easily impart a deeply rich coffee flavor. You can find espresso powder in some supermarkets, Italian markets, specialty and gourmet food stores, or online.

EXTRACTS

Most cookie recipes call for vanilla extract. Always use high-quality extracts, none of the imitation stuff.

NUTS

Nuts add lots of flavor and texture to cookies and other baked goods. Always be sure your nuts haven't gone rancid before using them. Store nuts in an airtight container in a dark, cool place in your pantry or in the freezer. Toasting nuts adds extra flavor.

PEANUT BUTTER

Avoid "natural" peanut butters that separate and require stirring. They simply don't bake well. The hydrogenated oil and emulsifiers added to conventional peanut butter truly do produce a better baking result. Whatever you like to eat, don't use a product made only from peanuts for baking. It will produce greasy, flat cookies.

SALT

Salt is used to bring out the sweetness and other flavors in baked goods. Without salt, even sweet things taste boring. Fine sea salt is a great option for baking and is what I used for testing the recipes in this book. You can also use table salt. If you use kosher salt in place of fine salt, you'll need to add a bit more, following the formula below.

1 teaspoon table or fine sea salt = 1¼ teaspoons kosher salt

Control Chocolate Chip Cookies

YIELD: about 26 large cookies

Below is the control chocolate chip cookie recipe, the recipe I used throughout the Cookie Customization and Cookie Troubleshooting chapters that follow to illustrate the various ingredients and techniques that make a surprisingly big impact on the final result.

I used the below recipe exactly but made one small change at a time to photograph (and taste!) the results, showing you how to customize or prevent failures. The recipe represents the most common and classic chocolate chip cookie recipe, which I felt made for a perfect base for experimenting.

2½ cups (317 grams) all-purpose flour

1 teaspoon baking soda

1 teaspoon baking powder

1 teaspoon salt

2 sticks (226 grams) unsalted butter, at cool room temperature

¾ cup (150 grams) granulated sugar

¾ cup (150 grams) lightly packed light brown sugar

2 large eggs, at cool room temperature

1 teaspoon vanilla extract

2 cups (340 grams) semi-sweet chocolate chips

1. Preheat the oven to 350°F. Line baking sheets with parchment paper.
2. In a medium bowl, combine the flour, baking soda, baking powder, and salt.
3. In the bowl of an electric mixer, cream the butter and sugars until light and creamy, 2 minutes. Add the eggs, one at a time, beating between additions. Add the vanilla, beat well to combine. On low speed, gradually beat in the flour mixture. Stir in the chocolate chips. Using a medium (1½-tablespoon) spring-loaded cookie scoop, drop the dough onto the prepared baking sheets.
4. Bake for 10 minutes, or until golden brown. Cool for 2 minutes before removing to wire racks to cool completely.

egg yolk
(chewy)
egg white
(cakey)
melted butter
(thin)
room temp butter
(thick)
corn syrup
(chewy)
cornstarch
(soft)
brown sugar
(thicker)
white sugar
(thinner)
cake flour
(cakey)
bread flour
(chewy)

3 CHAPTER | Cookie Customization

I am so excited for you to dive into this chapter. Using all of my cookie experiments and expertise, I have created this easy guide for you to use to customize *any* drop-style cookie recipe. Use it to create your ultimate cookie recipes—the cookies of your dreams! These will become your own perfected go-to recipes and everyone will beg you to share. Whether you're picturing the perfect cookie but can't get it quite right or you want to recreate your favorite bakery's recipe, this chapter includes everything you need to know to get the recipe just right. I will show you exactly what tweaks to make if you want your cookies to be chewy, soft, or cakey; thick and tall; thin and crisp; or just about everything in between! The tweaks are so simple and easy, you can do one or more and they can be mixed and matched. However, if you want to be a real cookie scientist, I advise changing only one thing at a time with every experimental batch.

If You Want Chewier Cookies . . .

To get more of that delightful chew so many of us crave in cookies, we need to not only add more protein but also more moisture. More protein creates more strands of gluten and the more gluten, the chewier the final result. Too much protein and gluten can make for a tough cookie, which is why we're adding extra moisture.

USE MORE BROWN SUGAR

How If your favorite cookie recipe calls for ½ cup brown sugar and ½ cup granulated sugar, bump it up slightly to ¾ cup brown sugar and ¼ cup granulated sugar. Dark brown sugar has even more moisture and flavor. Play around with this. As long as you keep the total amount of sugar the same, all should be delicious!

Why Brown sugar is very hygroscopic, which means it takes in and retains moisture. Conversely, granulated sugar is the least hygroscopic of the sugars, which leads to evaporation of moisture and therefore a crunchier cookie. Adding moisture to your cookie dough can help make it softer and chewier because it prevents gluten from forming. Not to mention the molasses in brown sugar will lend an incredible depth of flavor.

ADD AN EGG YOLK

How Add an egg yolk to just about any cookie dough recipe along with the other egg(s) called for. Note that since this does add extra moisture and increase spread, you may want to add in an extra tablespoon or so of flour if you prefer thick cookies.

Why In general, adding extra protein and fat to any cookie dough will lend more chewiness. Egg yolks contain all of the fat of an egg and just less than half of the protein, which makes it a perfect way to add chewy richness and flavor. Egg whites, conversely, can dry out baked goods. It also adds moisture, increasing the cookie's spread slightly while baking.

USE BREAD FLOUR

How Bread flour can be substituted for all-purpose flour on a 1:1 ratio. You can replace a portion, such as half of the flour in the recipe, or all of it, depending on how much chew you prefer. You can also add 30 seconds to the mixing time once the dough has come together to encourage more gluten development; just note that there is a fine line here between chewy and tough.

Why Using bread flour is the most effective way for adding protein to the dough. Bread flour has about 13 to 15 grams of protein per cup (depending on the brand) whereas all-purpose flour has about 10 to 12 grams per cup. This means more gluten creation and increased chew. Bread flour also often creates a thicker shape. Also, it can absorb more liquid than all-purpose flour, so more moisture will stay in the cookie!

CHILL THE DOUGH

How Give chilling a try. You can bake off a few cookies immediately if you must satisfy a craving (we've all been there!), but try chilling the dough for as long as possible, at least 24 hours or up to 72. Make it an extra delicious 3 days of experimenting by baking off a batch each day to compare the results.

Why Chilling cookie dough for 24 hours or longer produces some magical results. It gives the liquid in the egg a chance to hydrate the starch in the flour, making the dough firmer. And it allows the enzymes in the flour and egg yolk to break down the carbohydrates into its component sugars, fructose and glucose. Behind the veil of complicated science, chilling cookie dough makes the cookies much more flavorful, with that blissful caramelized butterscotch flavor, and it makes them thicker, chewier, and browner.

USE MELTED BUTTER

How Melt the butter before vigorously stirring in the sugar by hand and proceed with the recipe as normal, skipping the electric mixer altogether. If you want to reduce the spreading and greasiness the melted butter will cause, add an extra tablespoon or two of flour. Also, try combining melted butter with bread flour, because bread flour can absorb more liquid than all-purpose, keeping moisture inside the cookie!

Why Since butter is about 20 percent water, melting it first helps the butter mix together with the flour and form gluten. Remember the protein in flour needs liquid to form gluten, and more gluten means more chewiness.

ADD 1 TABLESPOON OF CORN SYRUP

How Add 1 tablespoon of corn syrup after creaming the butter with the other sugar in the recipe, beating until combined.

Why The addition of light corn syrup makes cookies noticeably chewier and less crispy. The long sucrose chains in corn syrup prevent the sugar in the dough from completely crystallizing. Plus, these chains are hygroscopic (like brown sugar), so they help your cookies stay softer longer.

If You Want Softer Cookies . . .

Generally, for softer cookies we want to add more moisture, more tenderizing ingredients, less protein, and heat them more gently.

USE MORE BROWN SUGAR

How If your favorite cookie recipe calls for ½ cup brown sugar and ½ cup white sugar, bump it up slightly to ¾ cup brown sugar and ¼ cup white sugar. Dark brown sugar has even more moisture and flavor. Play around with this, it won't make or break your cookies!

Why Brown sugar is hygroscopic, which means it takes in and retains moisture (much more than granulated sugar). Adding moisture to your cookie dough can help make it softer and chewier, and stay soft longer.

ADD CORNSTARCH

How Add 1 to 2 teaspoons, even a tablespoon if you're feeling bold, of cornstarch to any cookie recipe along with the other dry ingredients.

Why Cookies with cornstarch are ultrasoft and often slightly gooey and paler in color. As a thickening agent, it can also aid in lift and height.

USE PASTRY OR CAKE FLOUR

How Substitute pastry or cake flour for up to half of the all-purpose flour. Both pastry and cake flour, at about 4 ounces per cup, are slightly lighter than all-purpose, which is about 4½ ounces per cup. It's best to substitute based on weight measurements. Since there's less protein in these flours, the dough will develop less gluten and the cookies will spread relatively thin. You may want to add slightly more flour or chill the balls of dough before baking to prevent too much spreading.

Why Just like bread flour with its higher protein content (13 to 15 grams per cup) lends chewiness, pastry and cake flour with their lower protein content (about 8 grams per cup) lend softness. Cake flour is made from soft winter wheat and is extra finely ground, giving it an even softer, finer, more delicate texture.

ADD CREAM CHEESE

How Add ¼ to ½ cup (2 to 4 ounces) of room temperature regular-fat brick cream cheese to the butter and sugar in any cookie recipe, adding more or less depending on the yield of the recipe. You will need to add an additional 1 to 4 tablespoons of flour to compensate for the extra moisture. See the Snickerdoodle and Brown Sugar Cookie recipes that use cream cheese for inspiration (pages 164 and 125).

Why Not only does cream cheese add richness and an incredible depth of flavor, it also tenderizes the cookies so they're supersoft, even slightly chewy, without being cakey, due to the fat content.

BAKE AT 325°F

How Bake the cookies at 325°F, starting with the same length of time called for in the recipe. Slightly under-baked cookies will always be softer.

Why Cookies are usually baked at 350°F. Dropping the temperature creates a softer, less caramelized texture and flavor.

If You Want Cakey Cookies . . .

If more protein means more chew, less protein means less chew and a more delicate, tender, and cakey texture. That means using low-protein flour and not allowing the dough to develop much gluten. Mix the flour into the dough just until incorporated and not a moment longer to avoid too much gluten development.

The general ratio for a cakey cookie also involves less fat and sugar, ingredients that, in larger amounts, lead to more thin and crispy cookies. We also need more eggs because the water in them will evaporate while baking and produce steam. This will help the cookies rise while the protein in the eggs will coagulate and help keep that thicker shape. You can add an egg for a bit more cakey texture, or an egg white for a lot of cakey texture. Also keep in mind that the colder the dough is, the thicker the cookie will be.

ADD CORNSTARCH

How Add 1 to 2 teaspoons, even a tablespoon if you're feeling bold, of cornstarch to any cookie recipe along with the other dry ingredients.

Why Cookies with cornstarch are ultrasoft and often slightly gooey and paler in color. As a thickening agent, it can also aid in lift and height, making for a more cakey look and feel.

USE LIQUID SWEETENER

How Replace 15 to 50 percent of the sugar in the recipe with liquid sweetener. Any more than half and you may end up with a dry crumbly cookie because liquid sweeteners don't have a crystalline structure to hold air when beaten with butter. If you want to add just a touch of cakey softness, start with a tablespoon. You'll also need to increase the amount of flour since you're adding so much extra moisture. Start with about 2 tablespoons and work up to ½ cup if you're using a lot of liquid sweetener, gauging by the wetness of the dough. You'll have to play around with this as there's no exact ratio.

Why Liquid sweeteners, such as honey and maple syrup, are hygroscopic so they compete with the protein in the flour for moisture in the dough, slowing down the development of the gluten and creating more tender cookies.

ADD AN EGG WHITE

How Add an egg white to the other egg(s) called for in the recipe.

Why Unlike egg yolks, which add fat, egg whites add more water to the dough that eventually evaporates, creating a taller, lighter, more delicate, and slightly drier texture.

USE PASTRY OR CAKE FLOUR

How Substitute pastry or cake flour for up to half of the all-purpose flour. Both pastry and cake flour, at about 4 ounces per cup, are slightly lighter than all-purpose, which is about 4½ ounces per cup. It's best to substitute based on weight measurements. Since there's less protein in these flours, the dough will develop less gluten and the cookies will spread relatively thin. You may want to add slightly more flour or chill the balls of dough before baking to prevent too much spreading.

Why Just like bread flour with its higher protein content (13 to 15 grams per cup) lends chewiness, pastry and cake flour with their lower protein content (about 8 grams per cup) lend softness. Cake flour is made from soft winter wheat and is extra finely ground, giving it an even softer, finer, more delicate texture.

If You Want Thick and Tall Cookies . . .

To prevent the cookie dough from spreading and ensure it holds a thick and tall shape while baking, we need to keep the dough cold and reduce the moisture content. Anything we can do to prevent spread will help.

CHILL THE DOUGH

How Chill the dough for up to 72 hours in an airtight container, or refrigerate the balls of cookie dough until chilled, about 30 minutes to 1 hour, before baking.

Why Chilling cookie dough for 24 hours or longer produces some magical results. It gives the liquid in the egg a chance to hydrate the starch in the flour, making the dough firmer and resulting in less spread and more height while the cookies bake. You can also chill the balls of cookie dough so they are cold when they enter the oven, which will also result in slower spreading.

USE COLD BUTTER

How This will require more work from your electric mixer to cream the butter and the sugar, but should only take a few more minutes. Proceed with the recipe as normal.

Why Similar to the results from chilling the dough, the colder your ingredients are, the less spread will occur while the cookies bake. Use cold butter instead of room temperature butter to avoid over-spreading.

SCOOP TALL MOUNDS OF DOUGH

How Make the mounds as tall as you can, placing the baking pan in the oven carefully to avoid the mounds falling over.

Why Tall mounds will take longer to spread in the oven, resulting in a taller cookie.

ADD EXTRA FLOUR

How Add 1 to 4 tablespoons of extra flour, more if you want cookies that hardly spread.

Why Removing moisture from the dough by adding extra flour inhibits spreading while baking, resulting in a thick and tall cookie.

USE SHORTENING

How Replace half or all of the butter with shortening. I don't like to substitute the whole amount of fat because then you lose that buttery flavor and brown color.

Why Shortening has a higher melting point than butter and no water content, which means it will spread less while baking because it takes longer to melt and will moisten less. That's also why you should avoid adding additional water when replacing butter with shortening if you want thicker and taller cookies.

ADD CORNSTARCH

How Add 1 to 2 teaspoons, even a tablespoon if you're feeling bold, of cornstarch to any cookie recipe along with the other dry ingredients.

Why Since cornstarch is a thickening agent, it can aid in creating more lift and height in the baked cookies.

If You Want Thin and Crisp Cookies . . .

To promote spreading, we need more moisture. For crispness, we need moisture that will evaporate by the time the cookie is done baking. We also need things to be slightly warmer than usual for crispness and to begin the spreading process faster.

For thin and crisp cookies, the general ratio contains more fat, sugar, and chemical leaveners, which all contribute to spread. Granulated sugar is the least hygroscopic out of our typical sugar options and therefore leaves more moisture in the dough to evaporate while baking. This results in a crispy texture and thin shape. Use a lower-protein all-purpose flour here. Baking longer or at a higher temperature will also decrease the final moisture content and increase crunch.

USE MORE GRANULATED SUGAR

How Substitute granulated sugar for up to three-quarters of the total sugar in a recipe. Add additional granulated sugar beyond the total amount called for in the recipe for even more spread. Be wary of substituting all the sugar because if there's baking soda in the recipe it will need acid from brown sugar or other ingredients to activate (see page 59).

Why Use more granulated sugar than brown sugar to create flatter, crunchier cookies. While all sugars are hygroscopic, granulated sugar is far less hygroscopic than brown sugar or liquid sweeteners, meaning that it doesn't absorb as much moisture, resulting in increased spread and crispness. Even after a cookie dough is beaten and mixed, about half the sugar is yet to be dissolved. As the cookie bakes, that sugar finally dissolves, allowing the cookies to spread. The less sugar, the less spread.

ADD MILK

How Add a tablespoon or two of virtually any kind of milk with the eggs and vanilla. The dough should be slightly wetter and stickier.

Why Adding milk to the dough will increase the moisture and therefore the spread of the cookies.

USE LESS FLOUR

How Remove up to 3 tablespoons of flour from the recipe; the dough should be slightly wetter and stickier.

Why Again, this is about increasing the moisture content of the dough. If you have a big problem with your cookies not spreading, this is a great trick.

USE A HOT, GREASED BAKING PAN

How Place the baking pan in the oven for 5 minutes, or until hot, then spray with nonstick cooking spray.

Why More grease and heat means more spread. Once the dough hits the slick hot surface it begins to spread pretty much instantly.

USE MELTED BUTTER

How Melt the butter before vigorously stirring in the sugar. Let the mixture cool before proceeding with the recipe as normal. No need for creaming, as it's impossible with melted butter! This means you can skip the electric mixer altogether.

Why The warmer and more liquefied the butter is, the more it'll spread out in the oven.

BAKE THE COOKIES AT 375°F

How Raising the temperature even by 25 degrees to 375°F can result in a thinner, crispier cookie. You may want to shave a minute or two off the baking time.

Why In a hotter oven, the dough will begin to melt and spread more quickly and become more browned and crispy.

FLATTEN THE DOUGH

How Scoop the balls of dough out and then flatten them into discs with the palm of your hand or the bottom of a measuring cup.

Why Starting the cookie spreading before the dough hits the oven by flattening it does exactly what you'd think. It makes the dough more likely to spread out and flatten while baking.

Create Your Own Cookie Recipes

Developing your own cookie recipe is totally possible when you use my base as your foundation and everything you've learned about customization so far. When experimenting with your own recipes, it will likely take a few batches to get it just right. Bake off just a couple of cookies to start with so you can make tweaks and changes, like adding more flour or adjusting the baking time, without having to start over.

Basic Cookie Base Recipe

YIELD: about 20 cookies

This is a great starting place to create your own cookie recipe using the customization ideas in this chapter. It yields a smaller amount of cookies than many of the recipes in this book but can be easily doubled once you figure out your "formula."

1½ cups (191 grams) all-purpose flour

½ teaspoon baking soda

½ teaspoon baking powder

½ teaspoon fine sea salt

1 stick (113 grams) unsalted butter, at cool room temperature

¾ cup (150 grams) granulated sugar

1 large egg, at cool room temperature

½ teaspoon extract

1 cup mix-in

1. Preheat the oven to 350°F and line baking sheets with parchment paper.
2. In a medium bowl, whisk together the dry ingredients. Use an electric mixer to cream the butter and sugar for 2 to 3 minutes, until light and creamy, before beating in the egg and extract. Slowly add the dry ingredients, then stir in the mix-ins.
3. Using a medium (1½-tablespoon) spring-loaded cookie scoop, drop the dough onto the prepared baking sheets. Bake for 10 minutes, or until golden brown. Cool for 2 minutes before removing to wire racks to cool completely.

4 CHAPTER | Cookie Troubleshooting

I've said it many times and I'll say it again: baking is a science. With the following troubleshooting guide, complete with pictures for each problem, you can easily learn why your cookies don't turn out right without having to be a chemistry whiz. I've included every answer I could think of to the question, "what went wrong?"

We've all made at least one batch of cookies that look like one of the pictures in this chapter. Whether your cookies spread into sad flat puddles in the oven, or whether they became burnt or hard, or didn't spread at all, you now have all the answers you need to avoid those problems forever.

FLAT COOKIES

Was the butter too warm? If the butter is too warm and soft, it can cause the cookies to spread too much in the oven. This is due in part to it simply melting faster, but also because it couldn't maintain the air incorporated during the creaming process at its warmer temperature. If this has happened, your batch will, unfortunately, unavoidably turn out flat. Next time, use cool room temperature butter (65–67°F).

Was the dough too "wet"? Make sure you are correctly measuring your flour (see page 26) or try adding an additional one to four tablespoons of flour, especially if you live in a humid climate, at a high altitude, or have a gas oven.

Was the oven temperature too low? Be sure to thoroughly preheat the oven for at least 10 to 15 minutes before baking. Also, follow the directions on page 34 to ensure the oven temperature is correct.

Try chilling the balls of dough before baking in the fridge or briefly in the freezer.

Scoop tall mounds of dough instead of balls or disks to prevent too much spreading. You can also stack smaller scoops on top of each other to increase thickness.

Were the butter and sugar overbeaten? This may be the case if your cookies looked perfect in the oven but fell flat after cooling. Remember that you only need to beat for 2 to 3 minutes on medium-high speed. Overbeating can also cause the butter to warm too much and weaken its ability to hold air and the dough's ability to hold its shape.

Did you add too much or expired baking powder and/or baking soda? Too much chemical leavener can cause the cookies to deflate and expired leavener won't work at all to raise the cookies. See pages 59 and 60 for how to test the freshness of your leaveners.

If baking powder is called for, try using a different brand such as Argo, Bob's Red Mill, Clabber Girl, or Calumet.

Was the baking pan coated in too much nonstick cooking spray? Or lined with a silicone baking mat? This can cause the cookies to spread in the oven. Try parchment paper instead.

Was the baking pan hot from baking a previous batch of cookies? Be sure to use room-temperature baking pans. Bring pans to room temperature quickly by carefully running the bottom of the pan under cool water.

Replace a small portion of the flour with cornstarch to make for a firmer cookie that spreads less. Start with 1 tablespoon.

Try using half bread flour, which has higher protein content, in your dough. It will absorb more moisture, reducing spread.

Try using bleached flour, which generally soaks up more moisture than unbleached flour.

Try using more brown sugar than granulated sugar to reduce spread.

THICK COOKIES

Was the flour over-measured? Too much flour will reduce spreading. See the measuring tips on page 26 for correct flour measuring.

Was the amount of butter or other fat in the recipe reduced? Avoid changing the amount of fat in cookie recipes.

Were the butter and sugar properly creamed? Be sure to beat until the mixture is light in color and fluffy in texture, about 2 to 3 minutes. The mixture shouldn't be gritty.

Was the oven temperature correct? Be sure to thoroughly preheat the oven for at least 10 to 15 minutes before baking. Also, follow the directions on page 34 to ensure the oven temperature is correct.

Was a dark nonstick baking pan used? This can prevent the cookies from spreading.

Was the dough cold or even frozen? Sometimes if the dough is too cold the cookies won't spread.

Was a high-protein flour used? Try a flour with lower protein content.

Was shortening used? Try butter instead; its greater water content will increase spread.

Was the sugar reduced? Sugar liquefies with the heat of the oven to promote spread, so use the amount called for in the recipe.

TOUGH COOKIES

Was the dough overworked? Remember to mix the dry ingredients until just incorporated. Overmixing will create too many tough strands of gluten.

Was too much flour or too little liquid used? See page 26 on how to measure flour correctly.

Was high-protein flour used? Try using all-purpose or pastry flour, or a combination of the two.

Was the fat reduced? Was the sugar reduced? Avoid making these changes.

Were the cookies over-baked? Ensure accurate oven temperature with a thermometer and remove from oven after the minimum baking time, even before, because carryover cooking will continue to bake the cookies even after they're removed from the oven.

CRUMBLY COOKIES

Try mixing the final dough longer to make it cohesive by encouraging more gluten (gluten is like glue in cookie dough).

Use bread flour, which promotes gluten development, instead of all-purpose flour.

Add an additional egg yolk for moisture and binding power (egg whites can dry out cookies).

Was the chemical leavening overmeasured? Ensure all ingredients are accurately measured.

If you're making cookies with cocoa powder, try finding a cocoa powder with higher fat content. See page 62 for more information about cocoa powder.

UNEVEN COOKIES

Your oven may have hot spots. Be sure to rotate your pans halfway through baking or try baking only one sheet at a time in the center of your oven.

Your pan may not conduct heat evenly; use a high-quality thick and heavy aluminum pan.

Make sure you are scooping balls of dough that are as similar in shape and thickness as possible. Use a cookie scoop to do so.

BURNT COOKIES

Avoid using dark nonstick baking sheets, which promote browning and can lead to burning.

Only use the middle oven rack, anything too close to the heat source may cause burning.

Use an oven thermometer to ensure accurate cooking temperature.

Start checking on your cookies at the minimum baking time.

Remove the cookies from the cookie sheet and onto a wire rack 2 minutes after baking; the cookies will continue to cook on the hot pan.

Was too much sugar added to the dough? Try reducing the amount.

PALE COOKIES

Use fresh baking soda, which promotes browning (make sure there's some sort of acid in the dough, see page 59).

Was the sugar reduced? Use the amount called for in the recipe.

Use more brown sugar in the dough.

Don't use an insulated baking sheet, which will discourage browning.

The cookies may be undercooked, increase baking temperature and/or baking time slightly.

Check your oven temperature with a thermometer to make sure it's hot enough. Allow the oven to preheat for 20 minutes before baking.

BLAND COOKIES

Make sure to use the best quality ingredients possible and check for freshness.

Were the pans clean? Avoid transferring flavors by using clean pans and parchment paper.

Add an extra teaspoon of pure vanilla extract.

Use dark brown sugar for a more complex sweet flavor.

Chill the cookie dough for at least 24 hours to intensify the flavors.

Sprinkle the cookies with some sea salt after baking.

GREASY COOKIES

Add more flour to balance out the ratio of starch to fat. Start with 2 tablespoons and add up to ¼ cup, or enough to make the dough less sticky or greasy. Also make sure you're measuring correctly (see page 26).

Was the butter too warm? If the butter is too warm and soft it can cause the cookies to feel greasy or oily, so make sure it's at a cool room temperature (65–67°F) before using in the recipe. If the problem persists, try chilling the balls of dough before baking.

STALE COOKIES

Make sure the cookies are stored in an airtight container.

Add a piece of bread or tortilla to the container for storage.

Instead of storing, keep balls of cookie dough in the fridge for up to 3 days or in the freezer for up to 2 months and bake them off as desired.

PART II

So far in this book I've shown you every tip, trick, secret, and technique for successful cookie baking. Whether you learned how to fix your cookie frustrations or how to recreate a beloved family recipe, you now understand the building blocks of every cookie. Empowered with this information, you can approach any cookie recipe with confidence and even customize it to make it truly your own.

In the chapters that follow I have shared my most adored cookie recipes. These are tried-and-true favorites, the recipes everyone envies. In these recipes, the knowledge from the earlier chapters comes together to give you what I consider the "ultimate" version of each classic cookie. Everyone has different tastes and preferences, though, and you may prefer something slightly different. I encourage you to treat these recipes as foundations that you can explore, experiment with, customize, and revamp. You own the manual—now it's time to have fun with it!

Each recipe in this book has been tested many times, but if you run into any problems you can now use the troubleshooting guide (page 83) to get them just right. I've included variation ideas for many recipes to get the wheels turning, but there are limitless options for creativity. I hope you feel confident enough to be fearlessly imaginative in the kitchen. Here's to a more delicious life!

5 CHAPTER Chocolate Chip COOKIES

My obsession with cookies began with the classic chocolate chip, so it's only fitting to dedicate an entire chapter to this one cookie. You'll find variations on textures, shapes, sizes, and flavors here. If you're as obsessed as I am, thumbing back and forth from one recipe to another will help you to further understand the mad-cookie-baking science from the first half of the book.

Bakery-Style Chocolate Chip Cookies

YIELD: about 26 large cookies

In every way, these are quintessential chocolate chip cookies. They're one of the most popular recipes of all time on my website. You'll probably want to stock your freezer with this cookie dough *(see page 41)* *because once you've had one, the craving for them will return often!*

3 cups (381 grams) all-purpose flour

1 teaspoon baking soda

1 teaspoon fine sea salt

2 sticks (226 grams) unsalted butter, at cool room temperature

1¼ cups (250 grams) lightly packed light brown sugar

½ cup (100 grams) granulated sugar

2 teaspoons vanilla extract

2 large eggs, at cool room temperature

2 cups (340 grams) semisweet chocolate chips

1. If baking right away, preheat the oven to 350°F. Line baking sheets with parchment paper.
2. In a medium bowl, whisk together the flour, baking soda, and salt.
3. In a large bowl, use an electric mixer on medium-high speed to cream the butter and sugars until light and fluffy, 2 to 3 minutes. Add the vanilla and eggs, beating well after each addition. Slowly beat in the flour mixture. Stir in the chocolate chips with a rubber spatula.
4. If time permits, wrap the dough in plastic wrap and refrigerate for at least 24 hours but no more than 72 hours. Let dough sit at room temperature until it is just soft enough to scoop.
5. Using a large (3-tablespoon) spring-loaded scoop, drop balls of dough onto prepared baking sheets, spacing at least 2 inches apart.
6. Bake for 11 to 13 minutes, or until golden brown. Cool for 5 minutes before removing to wire racks to cool completely. Cookies can be stored in an airtight container at room temperature for up to 3 days.

Ultimate Chewy Chocolate Chip Cookies

YIELD: about 24 large cookies

These cookies are big, chewy, and loaded with butterscotch flavor. The higher hydration of this dough, compared to my Bakery-Style Chocolate Chip Cookies, coupled with the bread flour, egg yolk, generous portion of brown sugar, and the chilling time to "marinate" helps to create an intense chewy texture with an intense caramelized flavor.

1½ cups (191 grams) all-purpose flour

1¼ cups (159 grams) bread flour

1 teaspoon baking soda

1 teaspoon baking powder

1 teaspoon fine sea salt

2 sticks (226 grams) unsalted butter, at cool room temperature

1¼ cups (250 grams) lightly packed brown sugar

½ cup (100 grams) granulated sugar

2 large eggs plus 1 egg yolk, at cool room temperature

2 teaspoons vanilla extract

2 cups (340 grams) semisweet chocolate chips

1. In a medium bowl, whisk together the flours, baking soda, baking powder, and salt.
2. In a large bowl, use an electric mixer on medium-high speed to cream the butter and sugars until light and fluffy, 2 to 3 minutes. Add the eggs and egg yolk, one at a time, beating well after each addition. Beat in the vanilla. Slowly beat in the flour mixture. Stir in the chocolate chips.
3. Wrap the dough in plastic wrap and refrigerate for at least 24 hours but no more than 72 hours.
4. Preheat the oven to 350°F. Line baking sheets with parchment paper.
5. Let dough sit at room temperature until just soft enough to scoop. Using a large (3-tablespoon) spring-loaded scoop, drop balls of dough onto prepared baking sheets.
6. Bake for 12 to 15 minutes, or until golden brown. Cool for 2 minutes before removing to wire racks to cool completely. Cookies can be stored in an airtight container at room temperature for up to 3 days.

Soft Batch Chocolate Chip Cookies

YIELD: about 26 cookies

These cookies are ultra ooey and gooey with two special ingredients to keep them supersoft and tender: cornstarch and cream cheese! Your friends will love these cookies.

2¾ cups (349 grams) all-purpose flour

2 teaspoons cornstarch

1 teaspoon baking soda

1 teaspoon baking powder

1 teaspoon fine sea salt

10 tablespoons (141 grams) unsalted butter, at cool room temperature

¼ cup (57 grams) cream cheese, at cool room temperature

1¼ cups (250 grams) lightly packed light brown sugar

½ cup (100 grams) granulated sugar

2 large eggs, at cool room temperature

1½ teaspoons vanilla extract

2 cups (340 grams) semisweet chocolate chips

1. If baking right away, preheat the oven to 350°F. Line baking sheets with parchment paper.
2. In a medium bowl, whisk together the flour, cornstarch, baking soda, baking powder, and salt.
3. In a large bowl, use an electric mixer on medium-high speed to beat the butter, cream cheese, and sugars until light and creamy, about 2 minutes. Add the eggs, one at a time, beating well after each addition. Beat in the vanilla. Slowly beat in the flour mixture. Stir in the chocolate chips.
4. If time permits, wrap dough in plastic wrap and refrigerate for at least 24 hours but no more than 72 hours. Let dough sit at room temperature until it is just soft enough to scoop.
5. Using a medium (1½-tablespoon) spring-loaded scoop, drop balls of dough onto prepared baking sheets.
6. Bake for 10 minutes, or until barely golden brown. Don't overbake: the cookies will continue to cook from residual heat. Cool for 5 minutes before removing to wire racks to cool completely. Cookies can be stored in an airtight container at room temperature for up to 3 days.

Thin and Crispy Chocolate Chip Cookies

YIELD: about 20 cookies

Quick and easy, this recipe produces ultraslim, satisfyingly crunchy cookies just like your favorite high-end packaged brand. The only difference? Mine maintain a little chew just in the center. For the best results with this recipe, weigh your flour!

1⅓ cups (169 grams) all-purpose flour

½ teaspoon baking soda

¼ teaspoon fine sea salt

1 stick (113 grams) unsalted butter, melted and cooled

½ cup (100 grams) granulated sugar

⅓ cup (67 grams) lightly packed light brown sugar

2 tablespoons light corn syrup

1 large egg, at cool room temperature

1 tablespoon milk (any kind)

2 teaspoons vanilla extract

1 cup (170 grams) semisweet chocolate chips

1. Preheat the oven to 350°F. Line baking sheets with parchment paper.
2. In a medium bowl, whisk together the flour, baking soda, and salt.
3. In a large bowl, use a rubber spatula to vigorously stir the melted butter, sugars, and corn syrup until very well combined. Add the egg, milk, and vanilla and stir until very well combined. Gradually add the flour mixture and stir until just combined, being careful not to overmix. Gently fold in the chocolate chips. The dough will be very loose, sticky, and more like batter in consistency.
4. Using a medium (1½-tablespoon) spring-loaded scoop, drop balls of dough onto the prepared baking sheets, spacing at least 2½ inches apart.
5. Bake for about 12 minutes, or until golden brown and flat, rotating the sheets halfway through baking. Bake one sheet at a time for even cooking. When you remove the baking sheet from the oven, tap it against the counter.
6. Cool for 5 minutes before removing to wire racks to cool completely. Cookies can be stored in an airtight container at room temperature for up to 3 days.

TIP

These cookies will soften and become less crispy the longer they're stored.

To recrisp, heat the cookies in an oven heated to 350°F for 3 to 5 minutes, or until warmed through.

Thick and Cakey Chocolate Chip Cookies

YIELD: about 40 cookies

When you're craving a tall, fluffy, soft chocolate chip cookie that almost melts in your mouth, this is your recipe. Cake flour, cornstarch, and honey all help create that cakey texture.

- **2 cups (254 grams) all-purpose flour**
- **1 cup (113 grams) bleached cake flour**
- **1 tablespoon cornstarch**
- **1 teaspoon fine sea salt**
- **1 teaspoon baking powder**
- **¼ teaspoon baking soda**
- **2 sticks (226 grams) unsalted butter, at cool room temperature**
- **¾ cup (150 grams) granulated sugar**
- **¾ cup (150 grams) lightly packed light brown sugar**
- **1 tablespoon honey**
- **2 large eggs, at cool room temperature**
- **2 teaspoons vanilla extract**
- **2 cups (340 grams) semisweet chocolate chips**

1. Preheat the oven to 350°F. Line baking sheets with parchment paper.
2. In a medium bowl, whisk together the flours, cornstarch, salt, baking powder, and baking soda.
3. In a large bowl, use an electric mixer on medium-high speed to cream the butter, sugars, and honey until light and fluffy, 2 to 3 minutes. Add the eggs, one at a time, beating well after each addition. Add the vanilla. Slowly beat in the flour mixture. Stir in the chocolate chips. The dough will be slightly sticky.
4. Using a medium (1½-tablespoon) spring-loaded scoop, drop balls of dough onto prepared baking sheets, spacing 1½ inches apart.
5. Bake for 10 minutes, or until lightly golden brown. Cool for 5 minutes before removing to wire racks to cool completely. Cookies can be stored in an airtight container at room temperature for up to 3 days.

Coconut Oil Chocolate Chip Cookies

YIELD: about 28 large cookies

Not only does coconut oil offer a wonderful alternative to butter for those who can't enjoy dairy, it helps to create a mouthwatering tall, thick, and rich cookie. Measure the oil when it's solid but not rock hard at room temperature, about 70°F. Use refined coconut oil if you don't want any hint of coconut flavor.

1½ cups (191 grams) all-purpose flour

1¼ cups (159 grams) bread flour

2 teaspoons cornstarch

1 teaspoon baking soda

1 teaspoon baking powder

1 teaspoon fine sea salt

1 cup (210 grams) room temperature (solid) refined or virgin coconut oil

1¼ cups (250 grams) lightly packed light brown sugar

½ cup (100 grams) granulated sugar

2 large eggs plus 1 egg yolk, at cool room temperature

2 teaspoons vanilla extract

2 cups (340 grams) semisweet chocolate chips

1. In a medium bowl, combine the flours, cornstarch, baking soda, baking powder, and salt.
2. In a large bowl, use an electric mixer on medium-high speed to beat the coconut oil and sugars until very well combined, about 2 minutes. Add the eggs and yolk, one at a time, beating well after each addition. Add the vanilla. Gradually beat in the flour mixture. Stir in the chocolate chips with a rubber spatula.
3. Cover and chill the dough in the fridge for 30 minutes, or for up to 72 hours.
4. Meanwhile, preheat the oven to 350°F. Line baking sheets with parchment paper.
5. Using a large (3-tablespoon) spring-loaded scoop, drop balls of dough on prepared baking sheets.
6. Bake for 12-15 minutes, or until golden brown. Cool for 2 minutes before removing to wire racks to cool completely.
7. Cookies can be stored in an airtight container at room temperature for up to 3 days.

Chocolate Chip Graham Cracker Cookies

YIELD: about 25 cookies

This recipe contains no prepared graham crackers. Instead, the dough is made in the style of homemade graham crackers, studded with chocolate chips, and shaped into round cookies! Supersoft and chewy with a slightly craggy texture and distinct taste of graham crackers, they're a surprise favorite.

2½ cups (318 grams) all-purpose flour

¾ cup (150 grams) lightly packed dark brown sugar

1 teaspoon ground cinnamon

1 teaspoon baking soda

½ teaspoon fine sea salt

1 stick (113 grams) unsalted butter, cut into cubes and frozen

¼ cup (84 grams) honey

¼ cup whole milk

1 tablespoon vanilla extract

1 cup (170 grams) milk chocolate chips

1. In the bowl of a food processor, combine the flour, brown sugar, cinnamon, baking soda, and salt. Pulse one or two times to mix. Add the cubes of butter and pulse until the mixture resembles coarse meal.
2. In a liquid measuring cup, whisk together the honey, milk, and vanilla. Add the mixture to the food processor and pulse until a soft dough begins to form. Remove the food processor blade and stir in the chocolate chips with a rubber spatula. Shape the dough into a flat disk and wrap in plastic. Refrigerate until firm, at least 2 hours or overnight.
3. Preheat the oven to 350°F. Line baking sheets with parchment paper.
4. Using a medium (1½-tablespoon) spring-loaded scoop, drop balls of dough onto prepared baking sheets, spacing at least 2 inches apart. Flatten the dough balls with the bottom of a measuring cup.
5. Bake for about 12 minutes, or until the edges are browned. Cool for 5 minutes before removing to wire racks to cool completely. Cookies can be stored in an airtight container at room temperature for up to 3 days.

Brown Butter Chocolate Chip Cookies

YIELD: about 25 large cookies

Chewy, gooey, and crunchy goodness in every bite. I love to use chocolate chips and chocolate wafers here so you get those puddles of melty chocolate. Feel free to use only chocolate chips. You don't need an electric mixer for this recipe but you will need to refrigerate the dough for 24 hours before baking for best results.

2 sticks (226 grams) unsalted butter

1¼ cups (250 grams) lightly packed dark brown sugar

½ cup (100 grams) granulated sugar

1½ cups (191 grams) all-purpose flour

1 cup (127 grams) bread flour

1 teaspoon fine sea salt

1 teaspoon baking soda

¼ teaspoon baking powder

2 large eggs plus 1 egg yolk, at cool room temperature

2 teaspoons vanilla extract

1½ cups (255 grams) semisweet chocolate chips

1 cup (140 grams) semisweet chocolate baking wafers (Guittard or Valrhona)

1. Melt the butter in a small saucepan over medium heat. Continue to cook the butter, swirling the pan occasionally. It should become foamy and crack and pop audibly. When the crackling stops, continue to swirl the pan until the butter develops a nutty aroma and brown bits start to form at the bottom. Once the bits are amber in color, 2 to 3 minutes after the popping stops, remove from heat and pour into a mixing bowl. Add the sugars, stir, and set aside to cool completely.
2. In a medium bowl, whisk together the flours, salt, baking soda, and baking powder.
3. To the brown butter mixture, add the eggs, egg yolk, and vanilla and stir with a rubber spatula until combined. Slowly stir in the flour mixture until just combined. Stir in the chocolate chips and wafers.
4. Wrap the dough in plastic wrap and refrigerate for at least 24 hours but no more than 72 hours.
5. When ready to bake, let dough sit at room temperature just until it is soft enough to scoop.

6. Meanwhile, preheat the oven to 350°F and line baking sheets with parchment paper.
7. Using a large (3-tablespoon) spring-loaded scoop, drop balls of dough onto prepared baking sheets, leaving about 3 inches between each piece of dough to allow the cookies to spread.
8. Bake for 11 to 13 minutes, or until golden brown.

Peanut Butter Chocolate Chip Cookies

YIELD: about 24 large cookies

I absolutely adore this recipe because I absolutely adore peanut butter. The best part? You don't even need a stand mixer to get these perfect big, thick, chewy, soft cookies.

2½ cups (318 grams) all-purpose flour

1 teaspoon baking soda

1 teaspoon baking powder

1 teaspoon fine sea salt

1 stick (113 grams) unsalted butter

¾ cup (203 grams) creamy peanut butter (see tip)

1 cup (200 grams) lightly packed dark brown sugar

½ cup (100 grams) granulated sugar

2 large eggs plus 1 egg yolk, at cool room temperature

2 teaspoons vanilla extract

2 cups (340 grams) semisweet chocolate chips

1. Preheat the oven to 350°F. Line baking sheets with parchment paper.
2. In a medium bowl, whisk together the flour, baking soda, baking powder, and salt.
3. In a large heat-safe bowl, microwave the butter until melted. Vigorously stir the peanut butter into the hot butter with a rubber spatula until well combined. Stir in the sugars until well combined. Let cool if still hot.
4. Add the eggs and yolk, one at a time, stirring well after each addition. Add the vanilla. Slowly stir in the flour mixture. Stir in the chocolate chips with a rubber spatula.
5. Using a large (3-tablespoon) spring-loaded scoop, drop balls of dough onto prepared baking sheets, spacing at least 2 inches apart. Flatten dough slightly into disc shapes with your palms.
6. Bake for 12 minutes, or until golden brown. Cool for 5 minutes before removing to wire racks to cool completely.

TIP

Avoid using "natural" peanut butter with oil that separates from the solids. It's not a good choice for baking.

1 TEA SPOON
1 TABLESPOON
UNSALTED BUTTER
ORGANIC SWEET CREAM

6 CHAPTER | Classic COOKIES

Sometimes there's nothing better than the classics. It's my hope that in this chapter you'll find recipes you'll want to add to your baking repertoire and return to time and time again.

Peanut Butter Cookies

YIELD: about 28 cookies

Sometimes there's nothing better than a classic. For me, these soft and thick cookies invoke memories of sweet after school snacks. Feel free to put a creative spin on these traditional cookies. Use them to sandwich a layer of raspberry jam (or ice cream!) or drizzle them with melted chocolate.

2¼ cups plus 2 tablespoons (302 grams) all-purpose flour

1 teaspoon baking soda

¼ teaspoon baking powder

¼ teaspoon fine sea salt

1½ sticks (170 grams) unsalted butter, at cool room temperature

¾ cup (150 grams) lightly packed light brown sugar

¼ cup (50 grams) granulated sugar, plus ⅓ cup (67 grams) for rolling

¾ cup (203 grams) creamy peanut butter

1 large egg, at cool room temperature

½ teaspoon vanilla extract

1. Preheat the oven to 350°F. Line baking sheets with parchment paper.
2. In a medium bowl, whisk together the flour, baking soda, baking powder, and salt.
3. In a large bowl, use an electric mixer on medium-high speed to cream the butter, brown sugar, and ¼ cup of the granulated sugar until light and fluffy, 2 to 3 minutes. Beat in the peanut butter until well combined. Beat in the egg and vanilla. Slowly beat in the flour mixture.
4. Place the remaining ⅓ cup granulated sugar in a small bowl. Using a medium (1½-tablespoon) spring-loaded cookie scoop, divide the dough into balls. Roll between your palms to smooth, then coat in the granulated sugar before placing on the prepared baking sheets, spacing about 2 inches apart. Slightly flatten the dough by pressing the back of a fork into each ball of dough twice to create a crisscross pattern.
5. Bake for 10 to 12 minutes, or until the edges are slightly browned. Cool for 10 minutes before removing to wire racks to cool completely. Cookies can be stored in an airtight container at room temperature for up to 3 days.

Oatmeal Chocolate Chip Cookies (or raisins . . . if you must)

YIELD: about 24 cookies

This recipe is a keeper. Everyone goes crazy for these big, soft and chewy cookies loaded with gooey chocolate chips. Yes, you can swap out the chips for raisins if you insist. But serving these cookies with a tall glass of cold milk is a must!

1¾ cups (222 grams) all-purpose flour

1 teaspoon baking powder

½ teaspoon baking soda

½ teaspoon fine sea salt

¼ teaspoon ground cinnamon

1½ sticks (170 grams) unsalted butter, at cool room temperature

1¼ cups (250 grams) lightly packed dark brown sugar

¾ cup (150 grams) granulated sugar

2 large eggs plus 1 egg yolk, at cool room temperature

1 teaspoon vanilla extract

3 cups (297 grams) old-fashioned rolled oats

1½ cups (255 grams) semisweet chocolate chips

1. Preheat the oven to 350°F. Line baking sheets with parchment paper.
2. In a medium bowl, whisk together the flour, baking powder, baking soda, salt, and cinnamon.
3. In a large bowl, use an electric mixer on medium-high speed to cream the butter and sugars until light and fluffy, 2 to 3 minutes. Beat in the eggs, egg yolk, and vanilla, one at a time, beating well after each addition. Slowly beat in the flour mixture until just combined. Stir in the oats and chocolate chips with a rubber spatula.
4. Using a large (3-tablespoon) spring-loaded scoop, drop balls of dough onto prepared baking sheets. Flatten slightly with the bottom of a measuring cup.
5. Bake for about 14 minutes, or until the edges are slightly browned, rotating baking sheets halfway through. Cool for 5 minutes before removing to wire racks to cool completely. Cookies can be stored in an airtight container at room temperature for up to 3 days.

TIP

The acidic cream of tartar in this recipe is essential not just to offer that hint of tang, but also to give the cookies that distinct crinkly appearance.

Snickerdoodles

YIELD: about 18 large cookies

This recipe uses part butter and part coconut oil as a replacement for the traditional choice of shortening. The oil helps create a thick chewy cookie since, unlike butter, it contains no water. It also allows the cinnamon to shine. Choose refined coconut oil if you don't want any hint of coconut flavor.

2½ cups + 2 tablespoons (331 grams) all-purpose flour

3 teaspoons ground cinnamon, divided

1 teaspoon cream of tartar

½ teaspoon fine sea salt

¼ teaspoon baking soda

1 stick (113 grams) unsalted butter, at cool room temperature

½ cup (105 grams) refined coconut oil, solid

1¼ cups (250 grams) granulated sugar, plus ¼ cup (50 grams) for rolling

1 large egg plus 1 egg yolk, at cool room temperature

1 teaspoon vanilla extract

1. Preheat the oven to 375°F. Line baking sheets with parchment paper.
2. In a medium bowl, whisk together the flour, 1 teaspoon cinnamon, cream of tartar, salt, and baking soda to combine.
3. In a large bowl, use an electric mixer on medium-high speed to cream the butter, coconut oil, and 1¼ cups sugar until light and fluffy, 2 to 3 minutes. Add the egg, egg yolk, and vanilla and beat until combined. Slowly beat in the flour mixture.
4. Combine the remaining ¼ cup sugar and 2 teaspoons cinnamon in a shallow dish.
5. Using a large (3-tablespoon) spring-loaded scoop, divide the dough balls then roll in sugar to coat evenly. Place the dough balls on the prepared baking sheets, spacing 2 inches apart, and flatten with the bottom of a measuring cup. Sprinkle lightly with additional cinnamon sugar, if desired.
6. Bake for 10 to 12 minutes, or until the cookies set and begin to brown. Cool for 5 minutes before removing to a wire rack to cool completely. Cookies can be stored in an airtight container at room temperature for up to 3 days.

Soft and Chewy Sugar Cookies

YIELD: about 16 large cookies

This is my go-to drop-style sugar cookie recipe. It's one of those recipes that will become a part of your baking repertoire and that you will turn to for years to come. They're perfectly tender and soft with just the right amount of chewiness. If you want to make them festive and pretty without extra work, roll the balls of dough in colored sugar before baking.

2½ cups (318 grams) all-purpose flour

2 teaspoons baking powder

¾ teaspoon fine sea salt

2 sticks (226 grams) unsalted butter, at cool room temperature

1¼ cups (250 grams) granulated sugar, plus ¼ cup (50 grams) for rolling

1 large egg plus 1 egg yolk

1 teaspoon vanilla extract

1. Preheat the oven to 350°F. Line baking sheets with parchment paper.
2. In a medium bowl, whisk together the flour, baking powder, and salt to combine.
3. In a large bowl, use an electric mixer on medium-high speed to cream the butter and 1¼ cups sugar until light and fluffy, 2 to 3 minutes. Add the egg, egg yolk, and vanilla and beat until combined. Slowly beat in the flour mixture.
4. Place the remaining ¼ cup sugar in a shallow dish.
5. Using a large (3-tablespoon) spring-loaded scoop, divide the dough into balls, then roll in sugar to coat evenly. Place the dough balls on the prepared baking sheets, spacing 2 inches apart, and flatten with the bottom of a measuring cup.
6. Bake for 10 to 12 minutes, or until the cookies set and begin to brown. Cool for 5 minutes before removing to a wire rack to cool completely. Cookies can be stored in an airtight container at room temperature for up to 3 days.

White Chocolate Macadamia Nut Cookies

YIELD: about 28 large cookies

These big, round, golden brown cookies are dotted with buttery macadamia nuts and sweet white chocolate chips. They're a little crispy at the edges and slightly gooey in the center. Truly cookie perfection. Even people who don't like white chocolate will adore these!

- **3 cups (381 grams) all-purpose flour**
- **2 teaspoons cornstarch**
- **1 teaspoon baking soda**
- **1 teaspoon baking powder**
- **1 teaspoon fine sea salt**
- **2 sticks (226 grams) unsalted butter, at cool room temperature**
- **1 cup (200 grams) lightly packed light brown sugar**
- **½ cup (100 grams) granulated sugar**
- **2 large eggs plus 1 egg yolk, at cool room temperature**
- **2 teaspoons vanilla extract**
- **1½ cups (255 grams) white chocolate chips**
- **1½ cups (210 grams) chopped macadamia nuts**

1. If baking right away, preheat the oven to 350°F. Line baking sheets with parchment paper.
2. In a medium bowl, whisk together the flour, cornstarch, baking soda, baking powder, and salt.
3. In a large bowl, use an electric mixer on medium-high speed to cream the butter and sugars until light and fluffy, 2 to 3 minutes. Add the eggs and yolk, one at a time, beating well after each addition. Add the vanilla. Slowly beat in the flour mixture. Stir in the white chocolate chips and nuts with a rubber spatula.
4. If time permits, wrap dough in plastic wrap and refrigerate for at least 24 hours but no more than 72 hours. Let dough sit at room temperature until it is just soft enough to scoop.
5. Using a large (3-tablespoon) spring-loaded scoop, drop balls of dough onto prepared baking sheets, spacing at least 2½ inches apart.
6. Bake for 11 to 12 minutes, or until golden brown. Cool for 5 minutes before removing to wire racks to cool completely. Cookies can be stored in an airtight container at room temperature for up to 3 days.

Brown Sugar Cookies

YIELD: about 20 cookies

If you adore ultrachewy and slightly spiced cookies, this recipe is bound to become your new go-to. They may not look like a whole lot, but these cookies pack a huge flavor punch that will have everyone saying "Mmm, mmm!"

2 cups (254 grams) all-purpose flour

½ teaspoon baking powder

½ teaspoon ground cinnamon

¼ teaspoon baking soda

¼ teaspoon salt

¼ teaspoon ground ginger

¼ teaspoon ground nutmeg

1 stick (113 grams) unsalted butter, at cool room temperature

2 ounces (57 grams) cream cheese, at room temperature

1 cup (200 grams) lightly packed dark brown sugar

1 large egg, at cool room temperature

1 teaspoon vanilla extract

1. Preheat the oven to 350°F. Line baking sheets with parchment paper.
2. In a medium bowl, whisk together the flour, baking powder, cinnamon, baking soda, salt, ginger, and nutmeg.
3. In a large bowl, use an electric mixer on medium-high speed to beat the butter, cream cheese, and sugar until light and fluffy, about 3 minutes. Add the egg and vanilla and beat until combined. Slowly beat in the flour mixture.
4. Using a medium (1½-tablespoon) spring-loaded scoop, drop balls of dough onto prepared baking sheets, spaced at least 2 inches apart. Place on the prepared baking sheets and flatten with the bottom of a measuring cup to a 2-inch diameter.
5. Bake for 10 to 12 minutes, or until the cookies set and begin to brown. Cool for 5 minutes before removing to wire racks to cool completely. Cookies can be stored in an airtight container at room temperature for up to 3 days.

Raspberry Almond Thumbprint Cookies

YIELD: about 26 cookies

These buttery shortbread thumbprint cookies with a hint of almond flavor are filled with sweet raspberry jam and drizzled with a simple glaze. What I love most about this recipe? They look like beautiful prize gems on any cookie platter.

FOR THE COOKIES:

2 sticks (226 grams) unsalted butter, at cool room temperature

⅔ cup (133 grams) granulated sugar

1 teaspoon vanilla extract

½ teaspoon almond extract

2 cups plus 2 tablespoons (270 grams) all-purpose flour

¼ teaspoon fine sea salt

½ cup (160 grams) raspberry jam

TO MAKE THE COOKIES:

1. In a large bowl, use an electric mixer on medium-high speed to cream the butter and sugar until light and fluffy, 2 to 3 minutes. Add the vanilla and almond extract. Slowly beat in the flour and salt.
2. Shape the dough into a disc and wrap in plastic. Chill until firm, at least 4 hours.
3. When ready to bake, preheat the oven to 350°F. Line baking sheets with parchment paper.
4. Shape the dough into 1-tablespoon balls and place on prepared baking sheets, spacing about 2-inches apart. Make a small indentation with your thumb or the end of a spatula handle and fill with ½ teaspoon of jam. Freeze for 10 minutes, or until firm.
5. Bake for about 14 minutes, or until lightly browned at the edges. Cool on the baking sheets for 5 minutes before removing to a wire rack to cool completely.

FOR THE GLAZE:

1 cup (125 grams) powdered sugar

1 tablespoon milk

½ teaspoon almond extract (optional)

TO MAKE THE GLAZE:

1. Place a sheet of parchment paper underneath the cooling racks to catch the glaze for easier clean up. In a small bowl, whisk together the glaze ingredients. Transfer to a small zip-top bag and snip a very small hole in the corner. Use it to drizzle the glaze over the cooled cookies. Let set before serving.
2. Cookies can be stored in an airtight container at room temperature for up to 3 days or in the fridge for 1 week.

GHIRARDELLI
OREO

7 CHAPTER | Fun FLAVORS

Candies, spices, citrus, glazes, and sweet spreads, oh my! I hope you have as much fun baking the recipes in this chapter as I had dreaming them up.

Monster Cookies

YIELD: about 17 large cookies

Loaded with peanut butter, oats, chocolate chips, and M&M candies, these are a cookie monster's dream! They are one of my favorites to make around Halloween, but you can also make them festive for Christmas or Valentine's Day with different colors of M&Ms.

4 tablespoons (57 grams) unsalted butter, at cool room temperature

¾ cup (203 grams) natural creamy peanut butter, very well stirred

½ cup (100 grams) granulated sugar

½ cup (100 grams) lightly packed light brown sugar

1 large egg plus 1 egg yolk, at cool room temperature

1½ teaspoons vanilla extract

2 cups (198 grams) old-fashioned rolled oats

1 teaspoon baking soda

¼ teaspoon salt

½ cup (85 grams) semisweet chocolate chips

1 cup (200 grams) M&M candies

Flaky sea salt, optional, for topping

1. Preheat the oven to 350°F. Line baking sheets with parchment paper.
2. In a large bowl, use an electric mixer on medium-high speed to beat the butter, peanut butter, and sugars until light and fluffy, 2 to 3 minutes. Beat in the egg, egg yolk, and vanilla. Add the oats, baking soda, and salt, mixing on low speed until combined. Fold in the chocolate chips and M&Ms with a rubber spatula. The dough may be sticky.
3. Using a large spring-loaded scoop, measure out 3 tablespoon-sized balls of dough. Press the dough firmly into the scoop before placing it onto prepared baking sheets, spacing them at least 2 inches apart. Dough will be loose. Dot the tops of cookies with a few M&Ms and/or chocolate chips before baking for picture-perfect cookies.
4. Bake for about 13 minutes, or until the edges are slightly browned. Remove from oven and sprinkle flaky sea salt on top of the cookies, if desired. Cool for 5 minutes before removing to wire racks. For best texture and to allow the peanut butter flavor to fully develop, let cookies cool completely before serving.

Soft Lemon Poppy Seed Cookies

YIELD: about 20 cookies

If you could bottle up sunshine, this recipe would be loaded with it. Beautifully bright and refreshing, these glazed cookies are my go-to treat for warm sunny weather. Or, when you want to bring a little brightness to a gloomy cold day!

FOR THE COOKIES:

2 cups (254 grams) all-purpose flour

2 teaspoons baking powder

1 teaspoon cornstarch

½ teaspoon fine sea salt

10 tablespoons (141 grams) unsalted butter, at cool room temperature

1 cup (200 grams) granulated sugar

1 tablespoon fresh lemon zest (from about 2 medium lemons)

1 large egg plus 1 egg yolk, at cool room temperature

1 tablespoon honey

1½ tablespoons fresh lemon juice

2 tablespoons poppy seeds

MAKE THE COOKIES:

1. Preheat the oven to 350°F. Line baking sheets with parchment paper.
2. In a medium bowl, whisk together the flour, baking powder, cornstarch, and salt.
3. In a large bowl, use an electric mixer on medium-high speed to cream the butter, sugar, and lemon zest until light and fluffy, 2 to 3 minutes. Beat in the egg, egg yolk, and honey until well combined. Add the lemon juice and poppy seeds and mix until combined. Slowly beat in the flour mixture until just combined.
4. Using a medium (1½-tablespoon) spring-loaded scoop, drop balls of dough onto prepared baking sheets, spacing 2 inches apart. Slightly flatten dough with the bottom of a measuring cup.
5. Bake for about 12 minutes, or until cookies have just set and are slightly golden brown. Cool for 5 minutes before removing to wire racks to cool completely.

FOR THE GLAZE:

1 cup (125 grams) powdered sugar

1 tablespoon fresh lemon juice

Lemon zest, for garnish (optional)

Poppy seeds, for garnish (optional)

MAKE THE GLAZE:

1. In a small bowl, whisk together the powdered sugar and lemon juice until a thick glaze forms. Add more sugar or juice as needed to reach the desired consistency. Dip each cookie into the glaze. Sprinkle with zest and poppy seeds, if desired. Let the glaze set completely, about 20 minutes.
2. Store the cookies between layers of parchment paper in an airtight container at room temperature for up to 3 days.

Chai Sugar Cookies

YIELD: about 24 cookies

These easy Chai Sugar Cookies are thick, soft, loaded with sweet warm spices, and topped with a simple espresso glaze.

FOR THE COOKIES:

2 cups plus 2 tablespoons (270 grams) all-purpose flour

2 teaspoons baking powder

2 teaspoons ground cinnamon

1 teaspoon cornstarch

½ teaspoon fine sea salt

1 teaspoon ground cardamom

1 teaspoon ground ginger

½ teaspoon ground allspice

½ teaspoon ground cloves

10 tablespoons (141 grams) unsalted butter, at cool room temperature

1 cup (200 grams) granulated sugar

2 tablespoons honey

1 large egg plus 1 egg yolk, at cool room temperature

FOR THE GLAZE:

1¼ cups (156 grams) powdered sugar, sifted

2 tablespoons espresso or strong coffee

MAKE THE COOKIES:

1. Preheat the oven to 350°F. Line baking sheets with parchment paper.
2. In a medium bowl, whisk together the flour, baking powder, cinnamon, cornstarch, salt, cardamom, ginger, allspice, and cloves.
3. In a large bowl, use an electric mixer on medium-high speed to cream the butter, sugar, and honey until light and fluffy, 2 to 3 minutes. Beat in the egg and egg yolk. Slowly beat in the flour mixture until just combined.
4. Using a medium (1½-tablespoon) spring-loaded scoop, drop balls of dough onto prepared baking sheets, spacing 2 inches apart. Slightly flatten dough with the bottom of a measuring cup.
5. Bake for 12 minutes, or until cookies have just set and are slightly golden brown. Cool for 5 minutes before removing to wire racks to cool completely.

MAKE THE GLAZE:

1. Place a sheet of parchment paper underneath the cooling racks to catch the glaze for easier clean up. In a small bowl, use a small whisk or a fork to combine the powdered sugar and espresso until a thick but pourable glaze forms. Drizzle glaze all over cooled cookies. Allow to set. Store the cookies between layers of parchment paper in an airtight container at room temperature for up to 3 days.

S'mores Cookies

YIELD: about 32 cookies

What happens when you combine chocolate chip cookies and s'mores? Pure magic. Adding graham cracker crumbs to this dough gives the cookies a toothsome craggy texture while the chunks of gooey milk chocolate and sticky mini marshmallows on top make every bite pure heaven.

2 cups (254 grams) all-purpose flour

1 cup (142 grams) graham cracker crumbs, from 8 graham crackers

1 teaspoon baking soda

1 teaspoon fine sea salt

⅛ teaspoon ground cinnamon

2 sticks (226 grams) unsalted butter, at cool room temperature

1 cup (200 grams) lightly packed light brown sugar

¼ cup (50 grams) granulated sugar

2 large eggs, at cool room temperature

1 teaspoon vanilla extract

1 cup (170 grams) mini chocolate chips

1½ cups mini marshmallows

2 milk chocolate candy bars, chopped

1. Preheat the oven to 375°F. Line baking sheets with parchment paper.
2. In a medium bowl, whisk together the flour, graham cracker crumbs, baking soda, salt, and cinnamon.
3. In a large bowl, use an electric mixer on medium-high speed to cream the butter and sugars until light and fluffy, 2 to 3 minutes. Add the eggs and vanilla, one at a time, beating well after each addition. Slowly beat in the flour mixture. Stir in the chocolate chips with a rubber spatula.
4. Using a medium (1½-tablespoon) spring-loaded scoop, drop balls of dough onto the prepared baking sheets, spacing at least 2 inches apart.
5. Bake for 7 minutes, or until just beginning to set at the edges, and remove from the oven. Push 3 to 4 marshmallows and a few pieces of chocolate bar into each cookie. Return to the oven and bake for an additional 3 to 4 minutes, until the cookies are fully cooked. Cool for 5 minutes before removing to wire racks to cool completely.
6. Cookies can be stored in an airtight container at room temperature for up to 3 days.

Brown Butter Dulce de Leche Cookie Cups

YIELD: **48 mini cookie cups**

Pressing brown butter brown sugar cookie dough into the cavities of mini-muffin tins gives you the perfect vehicle for dulce de leche. Top with flaky sea salt and you have the perfect salty-sweet treat. You can find canned dulce de leche in the Latin aisle of many grocery stores, at specialty or gourmet food stores, or online.

1½ cups (191 grams) all-purpose flour

1½ cups (191 grams) bread flour

1 teaspoon fine sea salt

1 teaspoon baking powder

¼ teaspoon baking soda

2 sticks (226 grams) unsalted butter

1¼ cups (250 grams) lightly packed dark brown sugar

½ cup (100 grams) granulated sugar

2 large eggs plus 1 egg yolk, at cool room temperature

2 teaspoons vanilla extract

1 (13.4-ounce or 380 gram) can prepared dulce de leche

Flaked sea salt, for finishing

1. Preheat the oven to 350°F. Spray two 24-well mini-muffin tins with nonstick cooking spray.
2. In a medium bowl, whisk together the flours, salt, baking powder, and baking soda.
3. Melt the butter in a small saucepan over medium heat. Continue to cook the butter, swirling the pan occasionally. It should become foamy and crack and pop audibly. When the crackling stops, continue to swirl the pan until the butter develops a nutty aroma and brown bits start to form at the bottom. Once the bits are amber in color, 2 to 3 minutes after the popping stops, remove from heat and pour into a mixing bowl.
4. While the butter is still hot, stir in the sugars. Let cool before adding in the eggs, egg yolk, and vanilla, one at a time, stirring well after each addition. Gradually add in the flour mixture, stirring until combined.

5. Press tablespoon-size balls of dough into each muffin cup. Bake for 15 minutes, or until golden brown. Remove from the oven and use the handle of a wooden spoon or spatula to make 1-inch wide indentations into the center of each cookie.
6. Spoon a teaspoon of dulce de leche into each indentation. Sprinkle with sea salt. Let cool completely before serving. Cookies can be stored in an airtight container at room temperature for up to 3 days.

Cookies and Cream Cookies

YIELD: about 30 cookies

That's right, this recipe calls for crushed cookies inside the cookie dough! Each one is a little bite of ultrasoft and sweet satisfaction. They're particularly beloved by kids and practically require a cold glass of milk to accompany.

- **1¾ cups (222 grams) all-purpose flour**
- **1 teaspoon baking soda**
- **½ teaspoon salt**
- **1 stick (113 grams) unsalted butter, at cool room temperature**
- **2 ounces (57 grams) cream cheese, at room temperature**
- **½ cup (100 grams) granulated sugar**
- **¼ cup (50 grams) lightly packed light brown sugar**
- **1 large egg, at cool room temperature**
- **1 teaspoon vanilla extract**
- **12 chocolate sandwich cookies, coarsely crushed (see tip)**
- **¼ cup (43 grams) semisweet chocolate chips**
- **¼ cup (43 grams) white chocolate chips**

1. Preheat the oven to 350°F. Line baking sheets with parchment paper.
2. In a medium bowl, whisk together the flour, baking soda, and salt.
3. In a large bowl, use an electric mixer on medium-high speed to beat the butter, cream cheese, and sugars until light and fluffy, 2 to 3 minutes. Add the egg and vanilla and beat until combined. With the mixer on low speed, gradually add flour mixture, beating until combined. Stir in the cookie pieces, semisweet chocolate chips, and white chocolate chips with a rubber spatula.
4. Using a medium (1½-tablespoon) spring-loaded scoop, drop balls of dough onto prepared baking sheets, spacing at least 1½ inches apart. Flatten slightly with the bottom of a measuring cup.
5. Bake cookies for 8 to 10 minutes, or until the edges just begin to brown. Cool for 5 minutes before removing to wire racks to cool completely. Cookies can be stored in an airtight container at room temperature for up to 3 days.

TIP

To easily break up the chocolate sandwich cookies, place them in a large zip-top bag and smash them with a mallet or rolling pin. You want to have some large chunks remaining.

Red Velvet Cutout Cookies with Cream Cheese Frosting

YIELD: about 24 3-inch round cookies

These adorable cookies can be formed into any shape for a variety of holidays: hearts for Valentine's Day, stars for Fourth of July, or candy canes for Christmas! You can get festive with sprinkles and food coloring for the frosting as well.

FOR THE COOKIES:

3 cups (381 grams) all-purpose flour, plus more for dusting

¼ cup (21 grams) unsweetened cocoa powder

2½ teaspoons baking powder

⅛ teaspoon fine sea salt

1½ sticks (170 grams) unsalted butter, at cool room temperature

1½ cups (300 grams) granulated sugar

2 large eggs, at cool room temperature

2 teaspoons vanilla extract

1 teaspoon red gel food coloring

MAKE THE COOKIES:

1. In a medium bowl, sift together the flour, cocoa, baking powder, and salt.
2. In a large bowl, use an electric mixer on medium-high speed to cream the butter and sugar until light and fluffy, 2 to 3 minutes. Add the eggs, one at a time, beating until combined. Add the vanilla extract and food coloring, beating until thoroughly combined. Slowly beat in the flour mixture. Wrap the dough in plastic wrap, pat into a disk shape, and chill in the fridge until firm, about 1 hour or up to 2 days.
3. Line baking sheets with parchment paper. Place the chilled dough between two large pieces of parchment paper or plastic wrap on a work surface. Roll out to a ¼-inch thickness. If the dough is too firm, let it sit at room temperature for 5 to 10 minutes before rolling. Using a tall 3-inch round cookie cutter (or another shape of your choice) carefully cut out the dough and place the cookies on prepared baking sheets.
4. Chill baking sheets in the fridge for 30 minutes or until firm. Meanwhile, preheat the oven to 350°F.

FOR THE FROSTING:

- **4 ounces (113 grams) cream cheese, at room temperature**
- **4 tablespoons (57 grams) unsalted butter, at cool room temperature**
- **2 teaspoons vanilla extract**
- **1 cup (125 grams) powdered sugar, sifted (don't skip sifting!)**

5. Prick the dough all over with the end of an instant-read thermometer or the blunt end of a skewer. Bake for 10 to 11 minutes, or until the cookies are set. Cool on baking sheets for 5 minutes before removing to a wire rack to cool completely.
6. Unfrosted cookies can be stored in airtight containers at room temperature for up to 5 days or in the freezer for up to 1 month.

MAKE THE FROSTING:

1. In a large bowl, use an electric mixer on medium-high speed to beat the cream cheese, butter, and vanilla until very light, creamy, and smooth. With the mixer on low speed, gradually add the sugar and beat until fluffy.
2. Frost each cookie with a small offset spatula. Decorate with sprinkles if desired. Serve or store in an airtight container in a single layer, or between pieces of parchment paper, for up to 1 day.

8 CHAPTER | Chocoholic's DREAM

Every chapter in this book involves chocolate in some form or fashion, but this is where chocolate truly shines. I come from a long line of chocoholics and an ultimate cookie handbook just wouldn't be complete without a proper tribute!

Brownie Cookies

YIELD: **About 60 cookies**

An absolute crowd pleaser, these little cookies are exactly what you'd expect from the name: rich, fudgy, chewy, slightly gooey, and ridiculously chocolaty. In fact, there's a full pound of chocolate in this recipe!

1 pound (454 grams) semisweet baking chocolate, chopped

4 tablespoons (56 grams) unsalted butter

4 large eggs, cold

1¼ cups (250 grams) granulated sugar

1 teaspoon vanilla extract

½ cup plus 2 tablespoons (80 grams) all-purpose flour

1 teaspoon instant espresso powder (optional; see tip)

½ teaspoon baking powder

¼ teaspoon fine salt

1. In a large microwave-safe bowl, microwave the chocolate and butter in 30-second bursts, stirring between bursts, until melted. Let cool.
2. Whisk in the eggs, sugar, and vanilla. With a rubber spatula, stir in the flour, espresso powder (if using), baking powder, and salt. The consistency will be more like batter than dough. Cover and chill the batter in the fridge for an hour, or until firm.
3. Preheat the oven to 350°F. Line baking sheets with parchment paper.
4. Roll tablespoons of batter into balls and place on prepared baking sheets, spacing at least 2 inches apart. If the dough sticks to your hands as you roll, wet your palms with water.
5. Bake for 8 to 10 minutes, until crackled and firm on the outside. Be careful not to overbake—these cookies are meant to be fudgy and slightly gooey.
6. Cool for 5 minutes before removing to wire racks to cool completely. Cookies can be stored in an airtight container at room temperature for up to 3 days.

TIP

The espresso powder enhances the chocolate flavor without being noticeable. Omit it if you prefer, or increase it to a tablespoon for a mocha flavor.

Soft Triple Chocolate Cookies

YIELD: about 14 large cookies

This recipe is all about the chocolate. In fact, it includes three forms of it. The amount of chocolate far outweighs the butter to create an ultradense, rich, and sticky dough. These are the closest thing to fudge you'll ever see in a cookie. If you have a chocoholic in your life, bake them these cookies and they'll love you forever!

- 6 ounces (170 grams) semisweet baking chocolate
- 2 tablespoons (28 grams) unsalted butter
- 2 large eggs, at cool room temperature
- 2 tablespoons whole milk
- ⅓ cup (67 grams) granulated sugar
- ⅓ cup (67 grams) lightly packed light brown sugar
- 1 teaspoon vanilla extract
- 1 cup (127 grams) all-purpose flour
- ¼ cup (21 grams) unsweetened cocoa powder, sifted
- 1 teaspoon instant espresso powder (optional)
- ½ teaspoon baking powder
- ¼ teaspoon fine sea salt
- 1½ cups (255 grams) semisweet chocolate chips

1. Preheat the oven to 350°F. Line baking sheets with parchment paper.
2. In a medium microwave-safe bowl, heat the chocolate and butter in 30-second bursts, stirring between bursts, until melted and smooth. Allow to cool before stirring in the eggs, milk, sugars, and vanilla with a rubber spatula.
3. In a medium bowl, whisk together the flour, cocoa, espresso powder, baking powder, and salt. Add the flour mixture to the melted chocolate and stir until just combined. Gently fold in the chocolate chips. The dough will be wet and sticky.
4. Using a large (3-tablespoon) spring-loaded scoop, drop balls of dough onto prepared baking sheets. Flatten each ball slightly with wet hands.
5. Bake for 10 to 12 minutes, or until set but still gooey. Cool for 10 minutes before removing to wire racks to cool completely. Cookies can be stored in an airtight container at room temperature for up to 3 days.

Chocolate Crinkles

YIELD: about 18 cookies

These soft and fudge-like cookies are as beautiful as they are scrumptious. The dough is so rich it must be well chilled before it can be scooped and baked. Rolling the dough balls in powdered sugar twice truly does make all the difference!

- ½ cup (64 grams) all-purpose flour
- ½ cup (43 grams) unsweetened cocoa powder, sifted
- ½ teaspoon instant espresso powder (optional)
- 1 teaspoon baking powder
- ⅛ teaspoon fine sea salt
- 4 tablespoons (57 grams) unsalted butter, at cool room temperature
- ⅓ cup (67 grams) granulated sugar
- ⅓ cup (67 grams) lightly packed light brown sugar
- 2 large eggs, at cool room temperature
- 1 tablespoon milk
- 4 ounces (113 grams) semisweet baking chocolate, melted and cooled
- ½ cup (63 grams) powdered sugar, for rolling

1. In a medium bowl, sift together the flour, cocoa, espresso powder, baking powder, and salt.
2. In a large bowl, use an electric mixer on medium-high speed to cream the butter and sugars until light and fluffy, 2 to 3 minutes. Beat in the eggs, one at a time, and the milk until well combined. Beat in the cooled melted chocolate. Slowly beat in the flour mixture. Flatten dough into a disk, wrap in plastic, and freeze until firm, about 45 minutes.
3. Preheat the oven to 350°F. Line two baking sheets with parchment paper.
4. Using a medium (1½-tablespoon) spring-loaded scoop, drop balls of dough onto prepared baking sheets. Pour powdered sugar into a medium bowl and roll the dough balls in sugar two times, letting them sit in sugar between coatings. Place the cookies back on the prepared baking sheets, spacing 2 inches apart.
5. Bake until cookies have spread and coating is cracked, 12 to 14 minutes. Cool for 5 minutes before removing to wire racks to cool completely. Cookies can be stored in an airtight container at room temperature for up to 3 days.

Chocolate Hazelnut Sandwich Cookies

YIELD: 16 cookie sandwiches

These sandwich cookies are ultrarich and fudgy and loaded with tons of chocolate hazelnut flavor. You can also get creative with the filling and swap in peanut butter, marshmallow fluff, buttercream, or anything else you can imagine to make this recipe your own!

2½ cups (318 grams) all-purpose flour

½ cup (50 grams) Dutch-process cocoa powder, sifted

1 teaspoon baking soda

¼ teaspoon fine sea salt

1½ sticks (170 grams) unsalted butter, at cool room temperature

1½ cups (300 grams) granulated sugar

2 large eggs, at cool room temperature

2 tablespoons milk

2 teaspoons vanilla extract

½ cup (152 grams) chocolate hazelnut spread, for the filling

1. Preheat the oven to 350°F. Line baking sheets with parchment paper.
2. In a medium bowl, whisk together the flour, cocoa, baking soda, and salt.
3. In a large bowl, use an electric mixer on medium-high speed to cream the butter and sugar until light and fluffy, about 2 to 3 minutes. Add the eggs, one at a time, beating well after each addition. Add in the milk and vanilla and beat until just combined. Slowly beat in the flour mixture. The dough will be sticky.
4. Using a medium (1½-tablespoon) spring-loaded scoop, drop balls of dough onto prepared baking sheets, spacing at least 1½ inches apart.
5. Bake for 10 minutes, or until set. Cool for 5 minutes before removing to wire racks to cool completely.
6. Spread a tablespoon of chocolate hazelnut spread on the flat bottoms of half of the cookies, then sandwich them with the remaining cookies, bottom sides in. Cookies can be stored in an airtight container at room temperature for up to 3 days.

Gooey Chocolate Pizza Cookies

YIELD: two 6-inch pizza cookies

"Pure unadulterated indulgence" is the best way to describe this recipe. I love to use mini cast-iron baking dishes, but you can also use small pie plates or cake pans. Just keep an eye on them while baking; you may need to adjust the time slightly depending on the pan you use. We're aiming for underbaked and gooey here!

- 4 ounces (113 grams) semisweet baking chocolate, chopped
- 5 tablespoons (71 grams) unsalted butter
- ⅓ cup (67 grams) granulated sugar
- ⅓ cup (67 grams) lightly packed light brown sugar
- 1 large egg plus 1 egg yolk, at cool room temperature
- 2 tablespoons whole milk
- 1 teaspoon vanilla extract
- ¾ cup (95 grams) all-purpose flour
- ¼ cup (21 grams) unsweetened cocoa powder, sifted
- 1 teaspoon instant espresso powder (optional)
- ½ teaspoon baking powder
- ¼ teaspoon fine sea salt
- ⅔ cup (113 grams) semisweet chocolate chips
- Ice cream, for serving (optional)

1. Preheat the oven to 400°F. Spray two 6-inch pie plates or cast-iron baking dishes with nonstick cooking spray.
2. In a large microwave-safe bowl, heat the chocolate and butter in 30-second bursts, stirring between bursts, until melted and smooth. Stir in the sugars with a rubber spatula. Allow to cool slightly before stirring in the egg, egg yolk, milk, and vanilla until thoroughly combined.
3. In a medium bowl, whisk together the flour, sifted cocoa, espresso powder, baking powder, and salt. Add the flour mixture into the chocolate mixture and stir until just combined. Gently stir in the chocolate chips.
4. Divide the dough into two equal pieces and press into each prepared pan. You can cover the dough in the pan and refrigerate for up to 2 days before baking.
5. Bake for about 12 minutes, or until edges set but the inside is still gooey. Let cool for five minutes before serving—with ice cream, if desired.

Mint Chocolate Cookies

YIELD: about 25 cookies

I first made this recipe on a whim and didn't expect much. I brought them to my dad's house, and even years later he still requests I make a batch almost every time I see him. They're ultrarich and decadent and such a crowd pleaser, especially for those who love Andes Mints!

FOR THE COOKIES:

- 1¼ cups (159 grams) all-purpose flour
- ⅓ cup (28 grams) unsweetened cocoa powder
- 1 teaspoon baking powder
- ¼ teaspoon fine sea salt
- 1 stick (113 grams) unsalted butter, at cool room temperature
- ¾ cup (150 grams) lightly packed light brown sugar
- ¼ cup (50 grams) granulated sugar
- 3 ounces (85 grams) semisweet baking chocolate, melted and cooled
- 1 large egg plus 1 egg yolk, at cool room temperature
- ½ teaspoon vanilla extract
- 1 cup (150 grams) chopped Andes mint candies
- 1 cup (170 grams) semisweet chocolate chips

MAKE THE COOKIES:

1. Preheat the oven to 350°F. Line baking sheets with parchment paper.
2. In a medium bowl, whisk together the flour, cocoa, baking powder, and salt.
3. In a large bowl, use an electric mixer on medium-high speed to cream the butter and sugars until light and fluffy, 2 to 3 minutes. Add the melted cooled chocolate and beat until combined. Add the egg, egg yolk, and vanilla and beat until completely smooth and combined. Slowly beat in the flour mixture. Fold in the Andes mints and chocolate chips with a rubber spatula. The dough will be sticky.
4. Using a medium (1½-tablespoon) spring-loaded scoop, drop balls of dough onto prepared baking sheets, spacing 2 inches apart. Flatten slightly with the bottom of a measuring cup.
5. Bake for about 10 minutes, or until set. Cool for 5 minutes before removing to wire racks to cool completely.

FOR THE GLAZE:

1¼ cups (156 grams) powdered sugar, sifted

3 tablespoons milk

1 drop green gel food coloring, if desired

MAKE THE GLAZE:

1. Place a sheet of parchment paper underneath the cooling racks to catch the glaze for easier clean up. In a small bowl, use a small whisk or a fork to combine the powdered sugar, milk, and green food coloring, if using, until a thick but pourable glaze forms. Drizzle glaze all over cooled cookies. Allow to set. Store the cookies between layers of parchment paper in an airtight container at room temperature for up to 3 days.

Chocolate Cutout Sugar Cookies

YIELD: about 20 cookies

These cookies are a dream to work with and to eat. To make things easy, the soft dough is rolled out at room temperature and then refrigerated before you cut out shapes. Even after baking, these cookies hold their shape beautifully. And they have the perfect amount of chocolate flavor. I like to accentuate each cookie's shape with a simple border icing, but feel free to skip that step if you prefer.

FOR THE COOKIES:

2½ cups (318 grams) all-purpose flour

½ cup (50 grams) Dutch-process cocoa powder

1 teaspoon baking powder

¼ teaspoon fine sea salt

1½ sticks (170 grams) unsalted butter, at cool room temperature

1 cup (200 grams) granulated sugar

2 large eggs, at cool room temperature

1 teaspoon pure vanilla extract

MAKE THE COOKIES:

1. In a medium bowl, sift together the flour, cocoa powder, baking powder, and salt.
2. In a large bowl, use an electric mixer on medium-high speed to cream the butter and sugar until smooth and well combined, 2 minutes. Add the eggs, one at a time, beating until well combined. Add the vanilla extract. On low speed, gradually add the flour mixture and beat until thoroughly combined.
3. Place the dough between two large pieces of parchment paper or silicone mats on a work surface. Roll the dough out to a ¼-inch thickness. Chill in the fridge until firm, about 1 hour, or about 30 minutes in the freezer until firm.
4. Line large baking sheets with parchment paper. Use a 3-inch cookie cutter to cut out shapes from the dough and place on prepared baking sheets.
5. Gently reroll the scraps, cut out more shapes, and place on prepared baking sheets. If the sheet of dough softens too much at any point, place it back in the freezer or fridge until firm again before cutting and moving more shapes.

FOR THE ICING:

2 cups (250 grams) powdered sugar, sifted

2 to 3 tablespoons milk

¼ teaspoon vanilla extract

6. Chill the baking sheets of cut cookie dough in the refrigerator for 30 minutes or freezer for 15 minutes, or until dough is firm. Meanwhile, preheat the oven to 350°F.
7. Bake for 10 to 11 minutes, or until the cookies are set but not overbaked. Let cool on baking sheets for 5 minutes before removing to a wire rack to cool completely. Un-iced cookies can be stored in an airtight container at room temperature for up to 5 days or in the freezer for up to 1 month.

MAKE THE ICING:

1. In a medium bowl, whisk together the ingredients to form a thick and smooth icing. Add more milk if the icing is too thick, or more sugar if it's too thin.
2. Transfer the icing to a piping bag with a very small plain tip, a zip-top bag with a small hole cut in the corner, or a squeeze bottle. Outline the cookies with the icing. Allow to set before serving or storing. Cookies can be stored in an airtight container between layers of parchment paper at room temperature for up to 5 days.

9 CHAPTER | Bar COOKIES

I adore bar cookies. You don't have to wait for butter to come to room temperature, you typically don't need an electric mixer, and you don't have to spend time portioning the dough. Just melt some butter, add the other ingredients, plop into a baking pan, and bake! They're thicker and bigger and more substantial than traditional cookies and you can really have fun with flavors, fillings, and toppings.

Peanut Butter Chocolate Chunk Bars

YIELD: 9 large bars

If you love the combination of peanut butter and chocolate then this recipe was designed just for you. They're totally gooey and outrageously chewy. Feel free to add peanut butter chips, cups, or candies for an extra dose of PB goodness!

1 stick (113 grams) unsalted butter

1¾ (350 grams) cups light brown sugar

½ cup (135 grams) creamy peanut butter

2 large eggs plus 1 egg yolk, at cool room temperature

1 teaspoon vanilla extract

2¼ cups (286 grams) all-purpose flour

1 teaspoon baking powder

½ teaspoon salt

¼ teaspoon baking soda

6 ounces (170 grams) semisweet chocolate chunks, divided

1. Preheat the oven to 350°F. Line an 8-inch square metal baking pan with parchment or foil.
2. In a saucepan over medium heat, melt the butter. Add the brown sugar, stirring with a rubber spatula until smooth. Remove from the heat and stir in the peanut butter. Allow to cool.
3. Add the eggs and yolk, one at a time, stirring until well combined. Stir in the vanilla extract.
4. Add the flour, baking powder, salt, and baking soda. Stir to create a very thick dough-like batter. Fold in three-quarters of the chocolate chunks, reserving the rest for sprinkling on top.
5. Transfer the batter to the prepared pan and spread it evenly to the edges. Sprinkle with the remaining chocolate chunks and gently press them into the batter.
6. Bake for 30 minutes, or until the top is golden and the edges are slightly browned. Allow to cool in the pan. Use the parchment to remove the bars before cutting into squares and serving. The bars may sink slightly in the middle; this is normal. Store in an airtight container at room temperature for up to 3 days.

Caramel Peach Snickerdoodle Bars

YIELD: 9 large bars

Picture this: chewy cinnamon sugar cookie bars topped with ultragooey, soft, and perfectly ripe caramel peach topping. Every bite is the perfect combination of textures and flavors. Top with vanilla ice cream and it's pure bliss!

FOR THE BARS:

1½ cups (191 grams) all-purpose flour

1 teaspoon cream of tartar

1 teaspoon ground cinnamon

¾ teaspoon baking powder

¼ teaspoon baking soda

¼ teaspoon fine sea salt

1 stick (113 grams) unsalted butter, at cool room temperature

2 ounces (57 grams) cream cheese, at room temperature

½ cup (100 grams) granulated sugar

¼ cup (50 grams) lightly packed light brown sugar

1 large egg plus 1 egg yolk, at cool room temperature

1 tablespoon milk

1 teaspoon vanilla extract

MAKE THE BARS:

1. Preheat the oven to 350°F. Line an 8-inch square metal baking pan with parchment paper or foil, leaving an overhang on all sides.
2. In a medium bowl, whisk together the flour, cream of tartar, cinnamon, baking powder, baking soda, and salt.
3. In a large bowl, use an electric mixer on medium-high speed to beat the butter, cream cheese, and sugars on medium-high speed until well combined and smooth, about 2 to 3 minutes. Add the egg, egg yolk, milk, and vanilla, one at a time, beating well after each addition. Slowly beat in the flour mixture until combined.
4. Press the dough evenly into the prepared pan.
5. Bake for 25 minutes, or until lightly golden brown on top. Place the pan on a wire rack and let cool completely. Snickerdoodle bars without topping can be stored in an airtight container at room temperature for up to 3 days.

FOR THE TOPPING:

1 tablespoon unsalted butter

3 cups (420 grams) peeled, pitted, and sliced peaches (from about 4 to 5 peaches; thaw if using frozen)

¼ cup (50 grams) lightly packed light brown sugar

¼ cup (50 grams) granulated sugar

2 tablespoons all-purpose flour

½ teaspoon cornstarch

½ teaspoon fine sea salt

½ teaspoon ground cinnamon

½ teaspoon vanilla extract

2 tablespoons heavy cream

Vanilla ice cream for serving (optional)

MAKE THE TOPPING:

1. In a large skillet over medium-high heat, melt the butter. In a large bowl, toss the peaches and the remaining ingredients together. Add the peach mixture to the hot butter and cook, stirring often, until the mixture thickens, 6 to 8 minutes.
2. Top the bars with the warm peaches and vanilla ice cream, if desired, before serving.

Birthday Cake Confetti Cookie Bars

YIELD: 9 large bars

A birthday dream! (And so much easier to make and transport than a layer cake.) These thick and chewy confetti bars get a dose of extra flavor and soft texture from a bit of cream cheese. The almond extract in the buttercream frosting here is optional, but really helps convey that classic confetti cake flavor.

FOR THE BARS:

- **1¾ cups (222 grams) all-purpose flour**
- **1½ teaspoons cornstarch**
- **¾ teaspoon baking powder**
- **½ teaspoon baking soda**
- **¼ teaspoon fine sea salt**
- **1 stick (113 grams) unsalted butter, at cool room temperature**
- **2 ounces (57 grams) cream cheese, at room temperature**
- **¾ cup (150 grams) granulated sugar**
- **1 large egg plus 1 egg yolk, at cool room temperature**
- **1 teaspoon vanilla extract**
- **½ cup (75 grams) rainbow sprinkles, plus more for garnish**

MAKE THE BARS:

1. Preheat the oven to 350°F. Line an 8-inch square baking pan with parchment or foil, leaving an overhang on all sides. Spray with nonstick cooking spray.
2. In a medium bowl, whisk together the flour, cornstarch, baking powder, baking soda, and salt.
3. In a large bowl, use an electric mixer on medium-high speed to beat the butter, cream cheese, and sugar until light and fluffy, about 3 minutes. Add the egg, egg yolk, and vanilla and beat until well combined. Slowly beat in the flour mixture. Stir in the sprinkles with a rubber spatula until just combined.
4. Press the dough into the prepared pan.
5. Bake for 25 minutes, or until lightly golden brown on top. Place the pan on a wire rack and let cool completely.

FOR THE FROSTING:

1 stick (113 grams) unsalted butter, at cool room temperature

1¼ cups (156 grams) powdered sugar, sifted

2 to 4 tablespoons heavy cream

1 teaspoon vanilla extract

¼ teaspoon almond extract (optional)

⅛ teaspoon fine sea salt

MAKE THE FROSTING:

1. In a large bowl, use an electric mixer on medium-high speed to beat the butter until creamy, about 2 minutes. With the mixer on low speed add the powdered sugar, 2 tablespoons of cream, vanilla extract, almond extract, and salt. Increase speed to high and beat for 3 minutes, or until light and fluffy. Add more cream to thin the frosting or more powdered sugar to thicken it to your desired consistency.

2. Remove the bars from the pan using the parchment overhang. Frost with a thick layer of frosting. Garnish with sprinkles before cutting into squares. Serve or store in an airtight container at room temperature for up to 2 days or in the fridge for up to 5 days.

Caramel Pecan Blondies

YIELD: 9 large blondies

It truly doesn't get more decadent than this. These ultrachewy brown sugar blondies enrobe a hidden layer of rich, gooey, and crunchy caramel pecan filling. Prepared caramel candies make quick and easy work of this recipe. For the best results, use a metal baking pan and allow the blondies to cool completely before slicing.

FOR THE BLONDIES:

- 2 sticks (226 grams) unsalted butter, melted
- 2 cups (400 grams) lightly packed dark brown sugar
- 2 large eggs plus 1 egg yolk, at cool room temperature
- 1 tablespoon unsulfured molasses (optional)
- 1 teaspoon vanilla
- ¼ teaspoon fine sea salt
- 2 cups (254 grams) all-purpose flour

FOR THE FILLING:

- 25 (200 grams) soft caramel candies (such as Kraft brand), unwrapped
- 3 tablespoons heavy cream
- 1 cup (113 grams) pecans, chopped

1. Preheat the oven to 350°F. Line an 8-inch square baking pan with foil. Spray with nonstick cooking spray.
2. In a large bowl, combine the melted butter and sugar with a rubber spatula. Add the eggs, egg yolk, molasses (if using), and vanilla and stir until combined. Stir in the salt and flour.
3. Pour half the batter into the prepared pan.
4. Bake for 15 minutes, or until the top begins to set. Maintain oven temperature at 350°F.
5. Meanwhile, combine the unwrapped caramel candies with the cream in a microwave safe bowl. Microwave in 30-second bursts, stirring between bursts, until the mixture is melted and smooth. Stir in the pecans.
6. Pour the caramel over the partially baked blondie layer. Pour the remaining blondie batter over the caramel and spread to cover completely.
7. Return the pan to the oven and bake for another 30 minutes, or until golden brown and set. Let cool completely before cutting into bars. Blondies can be stored in an airtight container for up to 3 days. If desired, microwave the bars for 10 to 20 seconds before serving for a gooier texture.

Apple Crisp Cookie Bars

YIELD: **9 large bars**

As much as I love apple crisp, I always want it to have a more substantial bite. This recipe features a chewy brown sugar cookie base with an array of fresh cinnamon apples that are sprinkled with a crumbly, buttery oat crisp topping. Serve with vanilla ice cream for complete and utter dessert perfection!

FOR THE BARS:

1½ cups (191 grams) all-purpose flour

1 teaspoon ground cinnamon

½ teaspoon baking powder

¼ teaspoon baking soda

¼ teaspoon fine sea salt

1 stick (113 grams) unsalted butter

1 cup (200 grams) lightly packed dark brown sugar

2 tablespoons unsulfured molasses

1 tablespoon milk

1 large egg plus 1 egg yolk, at cool room temperature

1 teaspoon vanilla extract

MAKE THE BARS:

1. Preheat the oven to 350°F. Line an 8-inch square metal baking pan with parchment paper or foil, leaving an overhang on all sides.
2. In a medium bowl, whisk together the flour, cinnamon, baking powder, baking soda, and salt.
3. In a large microwave-safe bowl melt the butter in the microwave. While the butter is still hot, stir in the brown sugar with a rubber spatula. Allow to cool slightly before adding the molasses, milk, egg, egg yolk, and vanilla and stirring to combine. Gently stir in the dry ingredients.
4. Smooth the mixture into the prepared pan in an even layer. Partially bake for 17 minutes, or until the edges are just set but the center is still undercooked. Remove the crust from the oven and maintain the oven temperature at 350°F.

FOR THE APPLES:

2 small Granny smith apples, peeled, cored, and cut into ¼-inch slices

2 tablespoons granulated sugar

2 tablespoons heavy cream

1 teaspoon ground cinnamon

FOR THE OAT TOPPING:

⅓ cup (42 grams) all-purpose flour

⅓ cup (33 grams) old-fashioned rolled oats

¼ cup (50 grams) lightly packed light brown sugar

2 tablespoons (25 grams) granulated sugar

¼ teaspoon fine sea salt

3 tablespoons (42 grams) unsalted butter, cubed and chilled

Vanilla ice cream for serving

MAKE THE APPLE AND OAT TOPPINGS:

1. While the crust is baking, combine the apple ingredients in a medium-sized bowl. Set aside. Use a separate medium bowl to combine the flour, oats, sugars, and salt. Using a pastry blender or two knives, cut the butter into the dry ingredient mixture to form a coarse meal.
2. Once the crust has par-baked, carefully arrange the apple slices over the crust in one even layer. Sprinkle oat topping all over the apples.
3. Return the pan to the oven and continue baking until the topping is golden and the apples are soft, about 20 minutes. Allow to cool before slicing and serving. Top with vanilla ice cream, if desired.

Brown Butter Malted Toffee Cookie Bars

YIELD: Makes 6 bars

These bars are packed with so much unexpected flavor that your friends and family won't know what hit them!

1½ sticks (170 grams) unsalted butter, melted

1 cup (200 grams) packed dark brown sugar

2 teaspoons vanilla extract

1 large egg plus 1 egg yolk, at room temperature

¾ cup (95 grams) all-purpose flour

¾ cup (95 grams) bread flour

¾ cup (84 grams) malted milk powder

¾ teaspoon fine sea salt

¾ teaspoon baking powder

4 ounces (113 grams) semisweet baking chocolate, chopped into chunks

¾ cup (120 grams) chocolate toffee bits

Flaked sea salt, for sprinkling

1. Preheat the oven to 350°F. Line an 8-inch square metal baking pan with parchment or foil, leaving an overhang on all sides. Spray with nonstick cooking spray.
2. Melt the butter in a small saucepan over medium heat. Continue to cook the butter, swirling the pan occasionally. It should become foamy and crack and pop audibly. When the crackling stops, continue to swirl the pan until the butter develops a nutty aroma and brown bits start to form at the bottom. Once the bits are amber in color, 2 to 3 minutes after the popping stops, remove from heat. Stir the brown sugar into the hot butter. Let cool.
3. Add in the vanilla, egg, and egg yolk and stir until well combined. Gradually add in the flours, malted milk powder, salt, and baking powder and stir until just combined. Fold in the chocolate chunks and toffee bits, reserving some for sprinkling on top.
4. Press the dough evenly into the prepared pan. Sprinkle with the reserved chunks and bits, pressing down lightly with a spatula. Bake for 25 minutes, or until golden brown but not overcooked. Sprinkle with flaked salt. Cool completely before cutting into squares and serving. Bars can be stored in an airtight container at room temperature for up to 3 days.

Shortbread Squares

YIELD: **18 cookies**

Buttery, slightly sandy, and soft, these classic thick shortbread squares are perfect with a cup of coffee or tea. If you're a chocoholic like me, these squares are also great dipped or drizzled in chocolate!

1½ cups (191 grams) all-purpose flour

1 cup (99 grams) oats, old-fashioned or quick cooking

2 sticks (226 grams) unsalted butter, at cool room temperature

¾ cup (150 grams) lightly packed light brown sugar

½ teaspoon fine salt

1. Preheat the oven to 350°F. Line an 8-inch square baking pan with parchment paper or foil, leaving an overhang.
2. Place ingredients in the bowl of a food processor and process until a smooth, soft, sticky dough forms.
3. Press the dough into the prepared pan. Bake for about 25 minutes, or until lightly golden brown and set. Let cool in pan on a cooling rack.
4. Once cooled, remove the sheet of shortbread from the pan and cut into squares with a large, sharp knife. Cut each square into two triangles. Cookies can be stored in an airtight container at room temperature for up to one week.

10 CHAPTER | Holiday FAVORITES

To me there's nothing better than baking cookies around the Christmas and holiday season. That's why this is the largest recipe chapter in the book. For baking from Halloween to New Year's, you'll find a new recipe to try every weekend and holiday.

Pumpkin Chocolate Chip Cookies

YIELD: about 28 cookies

Finally, a pumpkin cookie that is soft and chewy instead of cakey! Pumpkin puree typically increases the moisture of cookie dough so much that the final result is cakey. This recipe takes advantage of bread flour, melted butter, and an egg yolk to create that chewy texture.

1½ cups (191 grams) bread flour

1 teaspoon ground cinnamon

½ teaspoon baking soda

¼ teaspoon fine sea salt

¼ teaspoon ground ginger

¼ teaspoon ground nutmeg

⅛ teaspoon ground cloves

1 stick (113 grams) unsalted butter, melted and cooled

¾ cup (150 grams) granulated sugar

¼ cup (50 grams) lightly packed light brown sugar

1 large egg yolk, at cool room temperature

1 teaspoon vanilla extract

⅓ cup (81 grams) pumpkin puree

1 cup (170 grams) semisweet chocolate chips

1. In a medium bowl, whisk together the flour, cinnamon, baking soda, salt, ginger, nutmeg, and cloves.
2. In a large bowl, combine the melted butter and sugars with a rubber spatula. Add the egg yolk and vanilla, stirring to combine. Stir in pumpkin puree until smooth. Add the flour mixture in three batches, mixing well after each addition, until a soft dough forms. Fold in the chocolate chips.
3. Cover and chill the dough in the fridge for 30 minutes, or until firm enough to scoop.
4. Meanwhile, preheat the oven to 350°F. Line baking sheets with parchment paper.
5. Using a medium (1½-tablespoon) spring-loaded scoop, drop balls of dough on the prepared baking sheets, spacing 2 inches apart. Flatten each slightly with the palm of your hand.
6. Bake for 10 to 12 minutes, or until set and edges are lightly browned. Let the cookies cool for 5 minutes before removing to a wire rack to cool completely. Store at room temperature in an airtight container for up to 5 days. The pumpkin flavor will intensify after a day.

Cranberry White Chocolate Chip Cookies

YIELD: about 28 large cookies

Perfectly big, thick, and chewy with crisp edges and soft centers, these cookies pack a flavor punch thanks to the tart cranberries, sweet and creamy white chocolate chips, and the hint of fresh orange zest.

3 cups (381 grams) all-purpose flour

1 teaspoon baking soda

1 teaspoon baking powder

1 teaspoon fine sea salt

1 teaspoon finely grated orange zest (optional)

2 sticks (226 grams) unsalted butter, at cool room temperature

¾ cup (150 grams) granulated sugar

¾ cup (150 grams) lightly packed light brown sugar

2 large eggs plus 1 egg yolk, at cool room temperature

2 teaspoons vanilla extract

¾ cup (86 grams) dried cranberries, chopped

1½ cups (255 grams) white chocolate chips

1. If baking right away, preheat the oven to 350°F. Line baking sheets with parchment paper.
2. In a medium bowl, whisk together the flour, baking soda, baking powder, salt, and orange zest, if using.
3. In a large bowl, use an electric mixer on medium-high speed to cream the butter and sugars until light and fluffy, 2 to 3 minutes. Add the eggs and yolk, one at a time, beating well after each addition. Add the vanilla. Slowly beat in the flour mixture. Stir in the cranberries and white chocolate chips with a rubber spatula.
4. If time permits, wrap dough in plastic wrap and refrigerate for at least 24 hours but no more than 72 hours. Let dough sit at room temperature just until it is soft enough to scoop.
5. Using a large (3-tablespoon) spring-loaded scoop, drop balls of dough onto prepared baking sheets, spacing 2½ inches apart.
6. Bake for 11 to 13 minutes, or until golden brown. Cool for 5 minutes before removing to wire racks to cool completely. Cookies can be stored in an airtight container at room temperature for up to 3 days.

Easy Cutout Sugar Cookies

YIELD: about 40 cookies, depending on shape and size

Unlike traditional cutout cookie recipes, here you roll out the cookie dough while it's soft and pliable, before chilling. Then you stamp out shapes from the cold dough with a cookie cutter. The result? Easy to make sugar cookies that maintain their shape perfectly! I've paired this recipe with easy cookie icing, which I find is simpler and tastier than royal icing.

FOR THE COOKIES:

3 sticks (339 grams) unsalted butter, at cool room temperature

1½ cups (300 grams) granulated sugar

2 large eggs, at cool room temperature

2 teaspoons vanilla extract

¼ to ½ teaspoon almond extract (optional)

4½ cups (572 grams) all-purpose flour

1 teaspoon baking powder

¼ teaspoon fine sea salt

MAKE THE COOKIES:

1. In a large bowl, use an electric mixer on medium-high speed to cream the butter and sugar until light and fluffy, about 3 minutes. Add the eggs, vanilla extract, and almond extract and beat until combined. Slowly add the flour, baking powder, and salt and beat until incorporated.
2. Divide the dough into 2 equal portions. Place one dough portion between two sheets of parchment paper and use a rolling pin to roll out to ¼-inch thickness. Repeat with the second portion of dough. Place the two sheets of dough on a baking sheet and chill for at least 1 hour or up to 1 day. You can also freeze the dough for 30 minutes.
3. Preheat the oven to 350°F. Line baking sheets with parchment paper.
4. Remove the dough from the fridge and cut into shapes with a cookie cutter, gently rerolling any scraps and cutting more shapes. Transfer the shapes to the prepared baking sheets. If the dough shapes are too warm to maneuver, freeze for 15 minutes or until firm.

continued

FOR THE BORDER ICING:

1 cup (125 grams) powdered sugar, sifted, plus more if needed

½ teaspoon vanilla extract

1–2 tablespoons milk

Food coloring, if desired

FOR THE FLOOD ICING:

1 cup (125 grams) powdered sugar, sifted, plus more if needed

½ teaspoon vanilla extract

2–3 tablespoons milk

Food coloring, if desired

5. Bake for 10 minutes, or until the cookies are set and very lightly golden at the edges. Be careful not to overbake them. Cool for 5 minutes before removing to a wire rack to cool completely. Baked un-iced sugar cookies can be frozen in an airtight container for up to 1 month.

FOR THE BORDER ICING:

6. In a small bowl, use a fork to beat together all the ingredients except the food coloring. Beat in the food coloring, a few drops at a time, until colored to your liking. The mixture should be very thick but still pourable. Add additional powdered sugar as needed.
7. Use a funnel to transfer the border icing to a squeeze bottle. You can also scoop it into a pastry bag fitted with a very small plain tip. Before you begin icing any cookies, take a few moments to practice on a piece of parchment paper to get the feel of the icing.
8. Holding the bottle or bag tip directly over one corner of a cooled cookie, begin tracing an outline of the cookie, squeezing gently and using both hands if needed to maintain consistent pressure. I prefer to allow a little slack in my icing stream as I go. If you mess up, simply wipe the icing off and start again. Allow the icing to dry slightly before continuing with the flood icing.

FOR THE FLOOD ICING:

9. In a small bowl, use a fork to beat together all the ingredients except the food coloring. Beat in the food coloring, a few drops at a time, until colored to your liking. The mixture should still be pretty thick, but will drizzle more freely than the border icing. If needed, add additional milk to loosen until the consistency is pourable. Pour the flood icing into a squeeze bottle or into a pastry bag fitted with a small plain tip.
10. Prepare as many batches and colors of flood icing as you need to decorate your cookies.
11. Begin filling the interior of the border drawn on each cookie with the flood icing, being careful not to add so much that it overflows the border. Use either the nose of the bottle or a toothpick to push the icing evenly over the cookie and up against the corners.
12. Leave the iced cookie to dry for 24 hours. The cookies are dry when the surface is completely smooth, dry, and resists smudging when touched. Store the dried cookies between sheets of parchment paper in an airtight container at room temperature for up to 10 days.

Peanut Butter Blossoms

YIELD: about 40 cookies

What's the holiday season without Peanut Butter Blossoms? They belong in every Christmas basket and are sure to delight Santa and his reindeer! Make these cookies even merrier by rolling them in green and red colored sugar.

FOR THE COOKIES:

2 cups (254 grams) all-purpose flour

1 teaspoon baking soda

¼ teaspoon baking powder

¼ teaspoon salt

1½ sticks (170 grams) unsalted butter, at cool room temperature

½ cup (100 grams) granulated sugar, plus ¼ cup (50 grams) for rolling

½ cup (100 grams) lightly packed light brown sugar

¾ cup (203 grams) creamy peanut butter

1 large egg, at cool room temperature

½ teaspoon vanilla extract

40 milk chocolate candy kisses, unwrapped, for finishing

1. Preheat the oven to 350°F. Line baking sheets with parchment paper.
2. In a medium bowl, whisk together the flour, baking soda, baking powder, and salt.
3. In a large bowl, use an electric mixer on medium-high speed to cream the butter and sugars until light and fluffy, 2 to 3 minutes. Beat in the peanut butter until well combined. Beat in the egg and vanilla. With the mixer on low speed, gradually add the flour mixture, beating until combined.
4. Place the remaining ¼ cup granulated sugar in a small bowl. Divide the dough into 1-tablespoon balls and roll in the sugar. Drop onto prepared baking sheets, spacing at least 1½ inches apart.
5. Bake for 10 minutes, or until lightly golden brown. Remove from the oven and immediately press a chocolate kiss into the center of each cookie. Cool on baking sheets for 5 minutes before removing the cookies to wire racks to cool completely. Cookies can be stored in an airtight container at room temperature for up to 3 days.

Gingersnaps

YIELD: about 22 cookies

Do you prefer crunchy, crisp, and thin gingersnaps or thick and chewy ones? I have excellent news for you. You don't have to choose! I've laid out the ingredients for both options below. Compare them side by side and see what differences you notice! The baking times for the two styles are slightly different, but otherwise the steps are the same.

CHEWY GINGERSNAPS (LEFT):

- 2¼ cups (286 grams) all-purpose flour
- 1½ teaspoons baking soda
- 1½ teaspoons ground ginger
- ½ teaspoon fine sea salt
- 1 teaspoon ground cinnamon
- ¼ teaspoon ground cloves
- 1 stick (113 grams) unsalted butter, at cool room temperature
- ½ cup (100 grams) granulated sugar, plus ½ cup (100 grams) for rolling
- ½ cup (100 grams) lightly packed dark brown sugar
- ⅓ cup (112 grams) unsulfured molasses
- 1 large egg, at cool room temperature

CRISPY GINGERSNAPS (RIGHT):

- 2¼ cups (286 grams) all-purpose flour
- 2 teaspoons baking soda
- 1½ teaspoons ground ginger
- ½ teaspoon fine sea salt
- 1 teaspoon ground cinnamon
- ¼ teaspoon ground cloves
- 1½ sticks (170 grams) unsalted butter, at cool room temperature
- ¾ cup (150 grams) granulated sugar, plus ½ cup (100 grams) for rolling
- ¼ cup (50 grams) lightly packed light brown sugar
- ⅓ cup (112 grams) unsulfured molasses
- 1 large egg, at cool room temperature

TIP

This recipe makes a perfect base for s'mores or ice cream sandwiches!

1. Preheat the oven to 350°F. Line baking sheets with parchment paper.
2. In a medium bowl, whisk together the flour, baking soda, ginger, salt, cinnamon, and cloves until combined.
3. In a large bowl, use an electric mixer on medium-high speed to cream the butter, sugar, and brown sugar until light and fluffy, 2 to 3 minutes. Add the molasses and egg and beat until combined. Slowly beat in the flour mixture.
4. Place the remaining ½ cup sugar in a shallow dish. Using a medium (1½-tablespoon) spring-loaded scoop, divide the dough into balls and roll in the sugar before placing on the baking sheet, spacing 2½ inches apart.
5. Bake for 13 minutes for chewy gingersnaps and 15 minutes for crispy ones, or until the tops are crackled. Cool on the baking sheets for 5 minutes before removing to cooling racks to cool completely. Cookies can be stored in an airtight container at room temperature for up to 3 days.

Biscotti

YIELD: about 24 cookies

Customize your own biscotti! Below is a basic biscotti recipe that you can use as the base for your own creations. Following the recipe are several flavor options, but feel free to get creative here. The possibilities are limitless.

1 stick (113 grams) unsalted butter, at cool room temperature

¾ cup (150 grams) granulated sugar

2 large eggs, at cool room temperature

2 cups (254 grams) all-purpose flour

1½ teaspoons baking powder

1. Preheat the oven to 375°F. Line a baking sheet with parchment paper.
2. In a large bowl, use an electric mixer on medium-high speed to cream the butter and sugar until light and fluffy, 2 to 3 minutes. Add the eggs, one at a time, and beat until just combined. Mix in the flour and baking powder to form a heavy dough.
3. Form the dough into a 13- by 3-inch log on the prepared baking sheet.
4. Bake for about 40 minutes, or until lightly golden brown. Remove to a wire rack to cool, maintaining the oven temperature at 375°F. Once cool enough to handle, use a sharp serrated knife to make ½-inch slices.
5. Place the slices cut side up on the baking sheet and bake for an additional 15 minutes, or until lightly toasted. Transfer to a wire rack to cool completely. Store biscotti in an airtight container at room temperature for up to 4 days or freeze for up to 3 weeks.

Biscotti Customizations

Chocolate Dipped

12 ounces (349 grams) chocolate, chopped (use any kind of baking chocolate you want)

Colored sugar, if desired

Place the chocolate in a microwave-safe bowl and microwave in 30-second bursts, stirring between bursts, until melted. Dip half of each biscotto into the melted chocolate and let the excess drip back into the bowl. Place on a baking sheet and sprinkle with sugar if desired. Refrigerate until the chocolate is firm.

Cranberry Pistachio

¾ cup (85 grams) pistachios, chopped

⅔ cup (76 grams) dried cranberries

1 teaspoon fresh lemon zest

Stir the mix-ins into the dough. You can also combine this variation with the one above and dip in white chocolate if desired!

Chocolate Peanut Butter

¼ cup (68 grams) smooth conventional peanut butter

½ cup (71 grams) dry-roasted peanuts

4 ounces semisweet baking chocolate, chopped into ¼ inch chunks

Beat the peanut butter in with the wet ingredients. After adding the dry ingredients, stir in the peanuts and chocolate chunks.

Cappuccino

1 teaspoon instant espresso powder

½ teaspoon ground cinnamon

1 cup (170 grams) milk chocolate chips

Stir the espresso and cinnamon in with the dry ingredients. Mix the chocolate chips into the dough.

Cinnamon Sugar

¼ cup (50 grams) granulated sugar

1 teaspoon ground cinnamon

Combine the sugar and cinnamon in a shallow dish. Sprinkle the just-sliced biscotti pieces with the cinnamon sugar before the final 15 minutes of baking.

Gingerbread

½ cup (100 grams) brown sugar

2 tablespoons unsulfured molasses

2 tablespoons all-purpose flour

2 teaspoons ground ginger

1 teaspoon ground cinnamon

½ teaspoon ground nutmeg

¼ teaspoon ground cloves

Decrease the ¾ cup granulated sugar in the base recipe to ½ cup and add ½ cup brown sugar. Add the molasses with the eggs. Add an additional 2 tablespoons flour and the spices along with the dry ingredients.

Anise

1 tablespoon anise extract

Add the anise extract with the wet ingredients.

Gingerdoodle Cookies

YIELD: about 22 cookies

What do you get when you combine a snickerdoodle and a gingersnap? Perfectly soft, chewy, and flavorful cookies that are the perfect addition to any Christmas cookie swap or gift box.

2¼ cups (286 grams) all-purpose flour

2 teaspoons ground cinnamon, divided

1½ teaspoons ground ginger

1 teaspoon cream of tartar

½ teaspoon fine sea salt

¼ teaspoon baking soda

¼ teaspoon ground cloves

1 stick (113 grams) unsalted butter, at cool room temperature

½ cup (100 grams) granulated sugar, plus ½ cup (100 grams), for rolling

½ cup (100 grams) lightly packed dark brown sugar

⅓ cup (112 grams) unsulfured molasses

1 large egg, at cool room temperature

1. Preheat the oven to 350°F. Line baking sheets with parchment paper.
2. In a medium bowl whisk together the flour, 1 teaspoon cinnamon, ginger, cream of tartar, salt, baking soda, and cloves.
3. In a large bowl, use an electric mixer to cream the butter, ½ cup granulated sugar, and brown sugar until light and fluffy, 2 to 3 minutes. Add the molasses and egg and beat until combined. Slowly beat in the flour mixture until combined.
4. Mix the remaining ½ cup granulated sugar with 1 teaspoon cinnamon in a shallow dish. Using a medium (1½-tablespoon) spring-loaded cookie scoop, shape the dough into balls. Roll in the cinnamon sugar before placing on the prepared baking sheets, spacing 2 inches apart. Flatten slightly with the palm of your hand.
5. Bake for 13 to 15 minutes, or until set. Cool on the baking sheets for 5 minutes before removing to cooling racks to cool completely. Cookies can be stored in an airtight container at room temperature for up to 5 days.

Spritz Cookies

YIELD: about 60 cookies

You don't need a cookie press to make beautiful Spritz cookies, just a large open star piping tip! Make these classic cookies even more festive by dotting the middle with a candied cherry, chocolate chip, or small spoonful of jam. Or use nuts, colored sprinkles, or colored sugars as decoration.

1 large egg yolk, at cool room temperature

1 tablespoon heavy cream

1 teaspoon vanilla extract

¼ teaspoon almond extract (optional)

2 sticks (226 grams) unsalted butter, at cool room temperature

⅔ cup (133 grams) granulated sugar

2 cups (254 grams) all-purpose flour

¼ teaspoon fine sea salt

1. Preheat oven to 350°F. Line baking sheets with parchment paper.
2. In a small bowl, whisk together the egg yolk, cream, vanilla, and almond extract, if using.
3. In a large bowl, use an electric mixer on medium-high speed to cream the butter and sugar until light, fluffy, and pale in color, 2 to 3 minutes. Add the egg yolk mixture, beating until thoroughly combined. Slowly mix in the flour and salt until just combined. Do not overmix or the cookies will be tough.
4. Fit a large reusable pastry bag with a ½-inch star tip (such as Ateco #846). Fill with the dough and twist to close. Pipe rosettes or swirls onto the prepared baking sheet about 2 inches apart. Garnish with sprinkles or colored sugars. If the dough is warm or soft, pop the baking sheet in the fridge or freezer until firm to the touch before baking.
5. Bake for 8 to 10 minutes or until lightly golden brown. Cool on baking sheets for 5 minutes before removing to wire racks to cool completely.

TIP

If the dough is too thick to pipe, either let it warm up slightly at room temperature or add an extra splash of heavy cream to loosen it up.

Brown Butter Pecan Pie Cookies

YIELD: about 24 large cookies

These cookies are thick with the perfect combination of soft and crunchy elements. There are a few extra steps involved, but I promise, it's so worth it. For an adult kick, add a tablespoon of bourbon to the cookie dough with the vanilla.

1½ cups (170 grams) chopped pecans

1½ cups (191 grams) all-purpose flour

1½ cups (191 grams) bread flour

1 teaspoon fine sea salt

1 teaspoon baking powder

¼ teaspoon baking soda

2 sticks (226 grams) unsalted butter, divided

1 cup (200 grams) lightly packed dark brown sugar

½ cup (100 grams) granulated sugar

2 large eggs plus 1 egg yolk, at cool room temperature

2 teaspoons vanilla extract

1. Preheat the oven to 300°F. Line a baking sheet with parchment paper and add the pecans in one even layer. Toast in the oven, stirring once or twice, until fragrant, 10 to 15 minutes.
2. In a medium bowl, whisk together the flours, the salt, baking powder, and baking soda.
3. Melt 12 tablespoons (1½ sticks) of the butter in a small saucepan over medium heat. Continue to cook the butter, swirling the pan occasionally. It should become foamy and crack and pop audibly. When the crackling stops, continue to swirl the pan until the butter develops a nutty aroma and brown bits start to form at the bottom. Once the bits are amber in color, 2 to 3 minutes after the popping stops, remove from heat and stir in the remaining 4 tablespoons of butter until melted.
4. Stir the sugars into the hot brown butter. Let cool. Add the eggs, yolk, and vanilla, stirring until combined. Gradually stir in the flour mixture. Stir in the toasted pecans.
5. Wrap the dough in plastic wrap and refrigerate for at least 24 hours but no more than 72 hours. Let dough sit at room temperature just until it is soft enough to scoop.

6. Preheat the oven to 350°F. Line baking sheets with parchment paper.
7. Using a large (3-tablespoon) spring-loaded scoop, drop balls of dough onto prepared baking sheets.
8. Bake for 12 to 15 minutes, or until golden brown. Cool for 2 minutes before removing to wire racks to cool completely. Cookies can be stored in an airtight container at room temperature for up to 3 days.

Gingerbread Cookies

YIELD: about 24 gingerbread men

A must-make every December, this recipe yields cookies that maintain their adorable shape but stay supersoft. This is a fun weekend project to do with your family. Get creative with cookie cutter shapes, icing designs, food coloring, and candy garnishes!

FOR THE COOKIES:

3 cups (381 grams) all-purpose flour

1¼ teaspoons ground ginger

1 teaspoon ground cinnamon

1 teaspoon baking powder

½ teaspoon baking soda

½ teaspoon fine sea salt

¼ teaspoon ground cloves

¼ teaspoon ground nutmeg

1½ sticks (170 grams) unsalted butter, at cool room temperature

½ cup (100 grams) lightly packed light brown sugar

½ cup (168 grams) unsulfured molasses

1 large egg, at cool room temperature

FOR THE ICING:

2 cups (250 grams) powdered sugar, sifted

2 to 3 tablespoons milk

¼ teaspoon vanilla extract

MAKE THE COOKIES:

1. In a medium bowl, whisk together the flour, ginger, cinnamon, baking powder, baking soda, salt, cloves, and nutmeg to combine.
2. In a large bowl, use an electric mixer on medium-high speed to cream the butter and brown sugar until light and fluffy, 2 to 3 minutes. Add the molasses and egg and beat until combined. Slowly beat in the flour mixture. Shape the dough into a thick disk and wrap in plastic. Refrigerate until firm, about 2 hours or up to 2 days.
3. Preheat the oven to 350°F. Line baking sheets with parchment paper.
4. Remove the dough from fridge and let stand until just warm enough to roll with ease. Place the chilled dough between two large pieces of parchment paper or plastic wrap on a work surface. Use a rolling pin to roll the dough to ¼-inch thickness. Use a gingerbread man or other cookie cutter to cut out shapes from the dough and place on prepared baking sheets, spacing at least a ½ inch apart. Gently reroll the scraps of dough to ¼-inch thickness and cut out more shapes.

5. If at any point the dough becomes too warm to hold its shape, return it to the fridge or freezer until firm again.
6. Bake for 10 to 12 minutes, or until the cookies set. Shave a couple minutes from the baking time if using smaller cookie cutters. Cool for 5 minutes before removing to wire racks to cool completely.

MAKE THE ICING:

1. In a medium bowl, whisk together the ingredients to form a thick and smooth icing. Add more milk if the icing is too thick, or more sugar if it's too thin.
2. Transfer the icing to a piping bag with a very small plain tip, a zip-top bag with a small hole cut in the corner, or a squeeze bottle. Decorate the cookies with the icing. Allow to set before serving or storing. Cookies can be stored in an airtight container between layers of parchment paper at room temperature for up to 5 days.

Russian Tea Cookies

YIELD: about 48 cookies

Also called Mexican wedding cakes, snowballs, or butterballs, these little morsels of heaven completely melt in your mouth. They're practically a requirement for any Christmas celebration!

2 sticks (226 grams) unsalted butter, at cool room temperature

1 cup (125 grams) powdered sugar, divided

1 teaspoon vanilla extract

2¼ cups (286 grams) all-purpose flour

¼ teaspoon fine sea salt

¾ cup (85 grams) finely chopped pecans, walnuts, or almonds

1. Preheat the oven to 375°F. Line baking sheets with parchment paper.
2. In a large bowl, use an electric mixer on medium-high speed to cream the butter, ½ cup powdered sugar, and vanilla until light and fluffy. With the mixer on low speed, gradually add the flour and salt. Stir in the nuts with a rubber spatula.
3. Shape the dough into 1-tablespoon balls and place on the prepared baking sheet, spacing 1 inch apart. Bake for about 9 minutes, or until the bottoms are lightly browned.
4. Remove the cookies from the oven and let cool for 1 minute. Place the remaining ½ cup powdered sugar for rolling in a deep mixing bowl. Roll the hot cookies in powdered sugar and let cool on a wire rack. Once cool, roll in the powdered sugar again. Cookies can be stored in an airtight container at room temperature for up to 3 days.

Turtle Thumbprint Cookies

YIELD: about 24 cookies

These cocoa cookies are rolled in chopped pecans, filled with salted caramel thumbprints, and drizzled with melted chocolate. This recipe is a little unique, so be sure to read through the steps before you start. Bakers beware: if you make this recipe once, you'll be asked to make it every holiday season!

FOR THE COOKIES:

1 cup (127 grams) all-purpose flour

⅓ cup (28 grams) unsweetened cocoa powder, sifted

¼ teaspoon fine sea salt

1 stick (113 grams) unsalted butter, at cool room temperature

⅔ cup (133 grams) granulated sugar

1 large egg, separated

2 tablespoons milk

1 teaspoon vanilla extract

1 cup (113 grams) pecans, finely chopped

FOR THE TOPPINGS:

16 (128 grams) soft caramel candies (such as Kraft brand), unwrapped

3 tablespoons whipping cream

Fleur de sel, or other flaked sea salt, for sprinkling (optional)

½ cup (85 grams) semisweet chocolate chips

1 teaspoon coconut oil or shortening

MAKE THE COOKIES:

1. In a medium bowl, whisk together the flour, cocoa, and salt.
2. In a large bowl, use an electric mixer on medium-high speed to cream the butter and sugar until light and fluffy, 2 to 3 minutes. Add the egg yolk, milk, and vanilla extract and beat until combined. Refrigerate the egg white in an airtight container until ready to bake. Slowly beat in the flour mixture.
3. Cover the dough and refrigerate until the dough is chilled and firm, about 1 hour or up to overnight.
4. Preheat the oven to 350°F. Line baking sheets with parchment paper.
5. Lightly beat the reserved egg white. Place the pecans in a shallow dish. Shape the dough into 1-inch balls. Dip each ball in the egg white, then roll in the pecans, pressing lightly to coat well. Place on the prepared baking sheet, spacing 1 inch apart. Lightly press down the center of each ball with your thumb or the handle of a wooden spoon or spatula.

6. Bake for 12 to 13 minutes, or until set. Set the baking sheet on a cooling rack and let cool for 5 minutes. While the cookies are warm, press down the center of each cookie again with your thumb or the handle end of a wooden spoon.

MAKE THE TOPPINGS:

1. Meanwhile, combine the caramel squares and cream in a small saucepan over low heat. Cook, stirring often, until the caramels are melted and the mixture is smooth.
2. Spoon about ½ teaspoon of caramel into each thumbprint cavity. Sprinkle the caramel with fleur de sel, if desired. Let cool completely.
3. In a small microwave-safe bowl, heat the chocolate chips and oil in the microwave for 1 minute. Stir until smooth. Transfer the chocolate to a zip-top bag and cut a small hole in one corner. Drizzle the chocolate over the cookies. Let the chocolate set before serving or storing in an airtight container at room temperature for up to 3 days.

Hot Cocoa Cookies

YIELD: about 20 cookies

This is certainly one of Santa's favorite recipes! For these cookies, hot chocolate mix and milk chocolate chips create a perfect base. Three-quarters of the way through baking, top each cookie with a piece of chocolate and half of a marshmallow for the ultimate gooey goodness. For picture-perfect results, use a kitchen torch to toast the marshmallow after baking.

1½ cups (191 grams) all-purpose flour

⅓ cup (32 grams) hot chocolate mix

1 teaspoon baking powder

½ teaspoon ground cinnamon

¼ teaspoon fine sea salt

1 stick (113 grams) unsalted butter, at cool room temperature

½ cup (100 grams) lightly packed light brown sugar

¼ cup (50 grams) granulated sugar

1 large egg plus 1 egg yolk, at cool room temperature

½ teaspoon vanilla extract

1 cup (170 grams) milk chocolate chips

8 ounces (227 grams) semisweet baking chocolate, cut into 20 equal pieces

10 large marshmallows, cut in half

1. In a medium bowl, stir together the flour, hot chocolate mix, baking powder, cinnamon, and salt.
2. In a large bowl, use an electric mixer on medium-high speed to cream the butter and sugars until well-combined and smooth, 2 minutes. Add the egg and egg yolk and beat until combined. Add the vanilla extract. Slowly beat in the flour mixture. Fold in the chocolate chips with a rubber spatula. Cover and chill for about 1 hour, or until the dough is no longer sticky.
3. Preheat the oven to 350°F. Line baking sheets with parchment paper.
4. Using a medium (1½-inch) spring-loaded scoop, drop balls of dough on prepared baking sheets.
5. Bake for about 10 minutes. Remove from oven and top each cookie with a piece of semisweet chocolate and 1 marshmallow half, cut side up. Return to the oven and continue to bake for 4 minutes, or until the marshmallows begin to melt slightly.

6. Remove from oven. Use a kitchen torch to toast the tops of the marshmallows. Alternatively, place the cookies under the broiler for about 30 seconds to toast the marshmallows. Be careful as the marshmallows can go from toasted to burnt very quickly!
7. Cool on baking sheets for 5 minutes before removing to wire racks to cool completely.
8. Cookies are best served the day they are made due to the marshmallows but may be stored in an airtight container in one flat layer for up to 3 days.

Ingredients Measuring Guide

Item	Measurement	Weight
Butter	½ cup/8 tablespoons/1 stick	113 grams
Chocolate chips	1 cup	170 grams
Cocoa powder	1 cup	85 grams
Coconut		
grated unsweetened	1 cup	113 grams
sweetened flakes	1 cup	85 grams
Coconut oil	1 cup	210 grams
Cream cheese	1 cup	225 grams
Flour		
all-purpose flour	1 cup	127 grams
bread flour	1 cup	127 grams
cake flour	1 cup	113 grams
Liquid sweeteners		
honey and molasses	1 cup	336 grams
maple syrup and corn surup	1 cup	312 grams
Milk	1 cup	227 grams
Nuts		
chopped/slivered	1 cup	113 grams
whole	1 cup	142 grams
Peanut butter	1 cup	270 grams
Pumpkin puree	1 cup	244 grams
Old-fashioned rolled oats	1 cup	99 grams
Sour cream	1 cup	227 grams
Sugar		
brown sugar	1 cup	200 grams
granulated sugar	1 cup	200 grams
unsifted powdered	1 cup	125 grams

Index

Acknowledgments

To my family for all of their love and support. To my mom for always encouraging me to pursue my dreams. To my dad for being my unofficial publicist wherever we go. To my brother Andrew for your enthusiasm. Thanks also to my dad and my grandma, Clara, for passing on the family sweet tooth.

To my best friend and fellow baker, Ashley Manila. You're my sister and your friendship means the world to me.

To all of my friends who are my cheerleaders and taste testers. Your excitement keeps me going!

To LeAnna Weller Smith. Not only are your designs absolutely beautiful, but you're very much the reason this book exists. Thank you for encouraging me to pursue this project and for helping me to navigate the path every step along the way.

To Ashley McLaughlin, who made nearly as many batches of cookies as I did to perfectly capture them in the mouthwatering photos throughout book. It was a tedious process to get everything just right, but I wouldn't have trusted it in the hands of anyone else!

To my editor Aurora Bell and proofreader Isabel McCarthy who whipped my writing into shape so meticulously and helped me to pull everything together.

To my Arizona dream team who make me feel fabulous in every portrait photoshoot: Lauren Hansen, Risa Kostis, Azure Schaffer, and Nicole Rehak Evans.

To my first Handle the Heat hire, Haley Wehner, for all of your beautiful designs and help managing social media and the community. I couldn't do it without you!

To my blogging and business buddies, this book also wouldn't exist without you. The support, ideas, encouragement, and friendship are what have given me the strength to pursue any idea, big or small.

To the Handle the Heat blog readers who have been asking for this cookbook for years. THANK YOU! You are the reason I do what I do. You are the reason I get to wake up daily to my absolute dream job. You are the reason this book was created. I'm forever grateful for your whole-hearted support and encouragement.